# Motivation

## Exercises to Decide What You Want and How to Get There

*(A Practical Guide to Unstick Yourself, Build Momentum and Sustain Long-Term Motivation)*

### Scot Johnson

I0558339

Published By **Andrew Zen**

**Scot Johnson**

*Motivation: Exercises to Decide What You Want and How to Get There (A Practical Guide to Unstick Yourself, Build Momentum and Sustain Long-Term Motivation)*

**ISBN 978-1-998927-22-7**

No part of this guidebook shall be reproduced in any form without permission in writing from the publisher except in the case of brief quotations embodied in critical articles or reviews.

Legal & Disclaimer

The information contained in this book is not designed to replace or take the place of any form of medicine or professional medical advice. The information in this book has been provided for educational & entertainment purposes only.

The information contained in this book has been compiled from sources deemed reliable, and it is accurate to the best of the Author's knowledge; however, the Author cannot guarantee its accuracy and validity and cannot be held liable for any errors or omissions. Changes are periodically made to this book. You must consult your doctor or get professional medical advice before using any of the suggested remedies, techniques, or information in this book.

Table Of Contents

# Chapter 1: What is Self-Motivation All About

How do you escape from mattress in the morning? Your brain tells you there are topics to be completed. Physically, your thoughts gives the instructions to your body to transport, that will help you get prepared for the day, however it's also the device that motivates you based totally on societal necessities.

As a little one, you studies from your mother and father that you want to get out of bed every day, accomplish every day duties, and be a effective part of society. The early gaining knowledge of system guarantees we attain maturity with self-motivation, however there are times on the same time because it breaks down.

We may furthermore experience depressed, dissatisfied, irritated, or do not have something better to do than sleep all day. Sometimes we do need to depend upon another individual to assist encourage us. But the truth is we furthermore want to have a deep self-motivation that ensures we're impartial of the help spherical us.

Self-motivation is defined through numerous dictionaries because the capacity to complete each day responsibilities, with out the help or have an impact on of a few other character or scenario. Those who are self-precipitated can discover a reason to be efficient, and the electricity to make sure subjects get completed, regardless of the stressful conditions or feeling that giving up can be plenty much less difficult.

Have you ever checked out someone and asked how does the man or woman get thru the day? When they've got this sort of busy schedule, how are they able to get everything completed with out truly seeking to give up?

It is their self-motivation. It is the capability to compartmentalize and interest at the obligations to be finished in preference to on the downsides or demanding situations.

Understanding what self-motivation is and the way it without a doubt works is the begin. You in the long run need to find out a way to advantage more self-motivation, which also stems from self guarantee.

Confidence and Self-motivation

How do you apprehend yourself? Do you agree with you studied you are sturdy? Can you control a few element that takes vicinity in the day or weeks ahead? Do you destroy down while subjects get a chunk difficult? Do you undertaking your feelings or movements onto others? Do you feel you are hiding your incapacity?

The above questions relate to self notion and how you apprehend yourself. There are a few those who keep going, doing, and in no manner seem to falter. Others talk down about themselves, but nonetheless accomplish lots. Some humans will project their emotions and it is the arrival of being "fine" that motivates them, at the same time as ultimately, they lack self assure.

Before you can begin to gain self-motivation and beautify yourself notion, you want to apprehend who you are and why you have to be working on the ones standards.

Why Learn to Motivate Yourself

We all have desires. When in depression, we on occasion overlook approximately those desires and accept as actual with we cannot accomplish them the least bit. We experience we are spinning our wheels, struggling, and likely it's far someone else's fault instead of our private. Have you had a warfare together with this? Are you in one now?

Depression is just one impact that might motive a lack of self-motivation and self assurance. For unique people, their youth route in no way gave them the choice to be prompted. Perhaps you constantly had someone to rely on, to motivate you to do matters, and that has persevered into adulthood.

Consider for a second that direction of the lady within the '50s. Many women had been delivered up with minimum schooling, knowledgeable they might no longer want university, however rather an etiquette college to learn how to be better halves, mothers and the house help for their strolling husbands. The concept that a few may go to college existed, however most often those were girls' schools supplying publications in art or education, and not regions like technological understanding and engineering. The motivation was typically about their husband and family. In the same vein, it additionally created severa struggles and sad moments.

The motivation for these ladies changed into primarily based mostly on their upbringing and what they had been recommended they will or couldn't gain. Think approximately how you will enjoy if your dad and mom cautioned you university have grow to be out of the query and all you can do become go to a trade school, marry, and raise children. How may you react? Perhaps, you have got been counseled this because it does however display up nowadays. You would probably have the mind that you need to trade this outlook, you want your youngsters to have more possibilities, and later in life you ultimately decide to do some thing to make modifications.

It isn't first-rate your responsibility to make certain the girl gender is regarded with equality, but some thing you ought to desire for your coronary coronary heart. We can all have the circle of relatives, glad marriage, and profession we need, if we're influenced enough to get it.

If you do now not want to sense caught within the '50s with just a few choices and a course that outcomes in an sad marriage, then you definitely need to take manage of your lifestyles and find out how you can inspire yourself.

Yes, upbringing is part of it. We do examine from our dad and mom, their perceptions, education and thoughts, but as a human with unfastened will, you in fact have the choice to decorate your life based without a doubt on your very private dreams. It doesn't be counted how prolonged it takes you to recognize the ones desires, what subjects is you're willing to strive.

Plenty of factors can get inside the way out of your upbringing to social perceptions, even your own biases. It goes to take stepping again and viewing your life, what you desire, and who you want to turn out to be earlier than you can discover motivation. It may additionally moreover take all the above to discover "why" you want to locate self-motivation.

Exercise for the 'Why'

Why are some ladies greater delivered about than others?

Consider Oprah for instance. She has risen to new heights in stardom, with performing in movies, walking her private talk display, her

TV channel, starting a mag, and writing books. What stimulated her? Interviews she has executed say she preferred to show that as a woman of African American historical past, it have end up viable to accumulate fulfillment, to help different women apprehend their capacity, and be an concept. She has honestly been all the ones topics.

Why could in all likelihood a lady try to harm her own family, despite the fact that she is divorced? What may also maintain motivating her to spend power on bad and adverse pathways? Money, hate, an lack of capability to truely love herself? There are high excellent and horrific reasons one may additionally moreover consider the usage of self-motivation in life. Before going into the workout, it is helpful to thing out that there may be a difference among self-motivation for development and high-quality emotions and the "poor" reasons you would possibly inspire your self into doing some thing.

It is time to discover "why" you need to discover self-motivation:

● What are your dreams?

● Do your goals enjoy practicable?

● How are you capable of select one dream and make it a fact?

● Are you sad together with your options in life?

● What are you able to do to alleviate the poor feelings and locate satisfactory emotions?

You do no longer want to have solutions to every question proper now. The concept is to discover who you are and why you've got were given have been given the desires or dreams that you preserve residing on.

You sought out a guide for self-motivation due to the reality some thing turned into making you sad. You are looking for a brand new way to technique lifestyles and acquire the dreams you preserve dwelling on. The exercising is requesting you to take the first step and write the desires down. When you could visualize them on paper, they emerge as greater real. It is likewise a way with the intention to have a have a look at the goals in complete and determine what's plausible to your current situation and what may also additionally need to change.

Often step one to finding extra motivation or any in any respect is to deal with why you are sad and what you could do to ensure a greater pleasant outlook. It takes time. For now, the "why" of gaining knowledge of self-motivation techniques are the maximum critical. As you float thru the guide, you may be given more sporting activities and facts that will help you advantage your desires.

How vital is Motivation

Self-motivation offers us with the capability to defend our pastimes. Without the mental manner of motivation, thru which we act, we'd not acquire our goals or dreams. Using motivation permits us to position away our weaknesses and supply attention to the strengths.

Motivation is quite vital to at least one's achievement. It offers:

- Commitment

- Personal Drive

- Optimism

- Initiative

Commitment comes into play when you have personal or profession related desires. Personal stress is all about the preference to meet goals, or perhaps exceed your requirements. Optimism allows you affirm life without the negatives maintaining you again. The initiative is the a part of motivation that helps you to be equipped for any opportunity that would present itself.

Those who're self-stimulated regularly consider, time manage skills, and are organized.

When assessing your motives for self-motivation, we noted societal preconceptions and pressures, which are extrinsic factors. To assist others, to be green to your career, even the comments of others may be motivating for you. The intrinsic factors are typically primarily based on feelings, together with love or the preference to have a look at thru. With "self" motivation being intrinsic you're more likely to perform an act for the pride it gives as opposed to extrinsic elements that name for satisfaction from others.

You can be stimulated in extraordinary approaches, the use of each intrinsic and extrinsic thoughts. What becomes of someone who isn't always self-prompted or even recommended is—properly—now not something. They do now not gain their desires, they spin their wheels within the equal useless-forestall jobs, and never gain happiness.

Motivation is crucial for numerous reasons:

● To experience love for yourself, and to truly receive it from others.

● To be glad for your life, and the options you are making.

● To lead through instance for contemporary generations.

● To acquire desires and desires you've got.

● To be capable of take the initiative on initiatives and opportunities.

● To live with a few problem, you begin and surrender it to the give up.

Without motivation, no longer some thing is probably finished. We would possibly now not have reached the moon, households couldn't have personal computers, automobiles would not be a issue, and the listing of innovations can cross on. No motivation equals a loss of safety, personal triumph, and fitness care while you suspect on a global scale.

You are geared up to maintain to your education approximately how the mind works, and the concept of neuroplasticity, in order to lead you to an information of the manner you could growth self-motivation no matter your age.

## Chapter 2: Neuroplasticity

Our brains are extremely good tools scientists do no longer virtually recognize. We are getting inside the path of attempting to discern out how the neural pathways artwork and the way it allows us suppose, react and manage our lives. The time period neuroplasticity is defined as the brains functionality to reform itself to create new connections on a neural degree. The neurons or nerve cells inside the mind can regulate at the equal time as crucial have to contamination, damage, or infection have an impact on the function. Neurons also can alternate responses for modifications or conditions.

Scientifically, the mind's functionality to reorganize uses axonal sprouting, in which undamaged axons will make bigger. These new axons form nerve endings that is probably severed due to infection, harm, or sickness. The new neural pathways fashioned ensure right characteristic takes place.

Let's say a mind harm occurs due to a car coincidence. The character is alive, but one hemisphere is broken. The healthful hemisphere will create new neural pathways to take over functions the opportunity hemisphere is unable to perform.

It should be cited that the type of concept does not generally paintings for the mind. Individuals who be afflicted by dementia or Alzheimer's have the form of brain ailment the contemporary-day axons are not able to form, and because of this new pathways cannot be created for the proper feature of the mind. With dementia it's miles approximately dropping mind period, for that reason neural pathways can not be formed.

When it entails self-motivation, neuroplasticity is an immensely useful concept. You can advantage from axons being formed to help redirect your conduct and thoughts characteristic. Experts moreover test with neuroplasticity as mind plasticity and mind malleability.

Since our primary state of affairs is self-motivation and reading strategies that will help you benefit motivation you haven't had in advance than, mind malleability is a better term. It suggests the capacity of the brain to conform as you need it to, therefore displaying you that you are malleable to data and mind restructuring.

Even even though the mysteries of the brain exist, we do understand the brain is a powerful computer. It is the laptop that allows us expect, do, and achieve achievement. You just need to retrain it to house the concept of self-motivation.

It will take time, repetition, and thoughts carrying sports activities to fulfill your goals.

The Brain

To understand the ideas of Neuroplasticity, you ought to apprehend more about the mind and its factors. Our brains are the maximum crucial of all vertebrates when it comes to body period. The regular thoughts weighs a hint over 3 pounds. The male mind is said to have a quantity of one,274 cubic centimeters, whilst the woman has 1,131 cubic centimeters. We additionally recognize the thoughts is set 2 percent of our body weight, and the cerebrum is in which 80 5 percentage of the load comes from.

We have 86 billion nerve cells or neurons, which anatomists discuss with as grey depend. In discussing neuroplasticity, we pointed out new neurons being long-established, so believe if genuinely one in every of your 86 billion nerve cells might not paintings and you're able to create a new one, plus a present day nerve fiber. Our brains have billions of nerve fibers crafted from axons and dendrites, which is the white matter within the mind. The neurons connect with trillions of synapses for physical characteristic. Even even as we sleep our mind is functioning to keep us respiratory, to repair harm to regions of the body and further.

From the spinal wire, there may be the brain stem, which connects to the opportunity sections of the mind. In anatomy, the various layers are known as the Basal Ganglia, Dura, Cerebellum, Cortex, Cranium (cranium), occipital lobe, parietal lobe, temporal lobe, and frontal lobe. You actually have a left and right hemisphere, which is wherein the left and proper mind concept is derived.

The lobes and the cortex are critical for self-motivation. The cortex is the area wherein questioning and voluntary actions start. The frontal lobes assist with problem solving, motor characteristic, and judgment. The parietal lobes help control frame role, handwriting, and sensations or emotions. Temporal lobes are wherein memory and taking note of are managed. The occipital lobes machine visible information. Even if you are picturing some element that isn't always inside the the front of you, the occipital lobes help your mind "see" what you are thinking about.

From the concise clarification you can tell there are various factors to brain function, it's miles why your complete brain desires to paintings efficaciously to make sure you're performing at an simplest degree.

While the brain is greater scientific and difficult era in relation, you moreover mght have the look at of psychology an awesome manner to allow you to understand the difference for your feelings, emotions, reactions and preferred overall performance. Before talking approximately the psychology of things, we are able to take a look at the ten ideas of neuroplasticity.

10 Principles of Neuroplasticity

Using neuroplasticity as a treatment technique, in which you have bodily video games to assist your mind create new thinking patterns, calls for an information of the 10 necessities in the back of the remedy gadget. The concept that neuroplasticity, which can be very technological information orientated, can be used to reprogram the mind isn't always a present day intellectual treatment treatment. The sporting activities are designed to use the mind's skills to offer better results. Here are the 10 mind.

1.Use features or you may lose the capability to

2.Use the capabilities and enhance upon them

three.Repeat, don't absolutely have a examine some trouble, but use repetition to form new exercises.

four.Be precise, even as you retrain your thoughts, use the same vocabulary to help you conquer.

five.Use severe schooling.

6.When someone is improving, it's miles identified that severa types of plasticity upward thrust up at numerous instances of day for the thoughts, that is why time topics while you are attempting to reprogram your belief approach.

7.Salience is on the equal time as an motion is tied to an movement or word that subjects to you especially. In hypnosis, to get someone to stop smoking, a good buy can be made, at the facet of waking up at 4 a.M. Every morning to avoid the yearning of smoking.

eight.Age goes to rely, however it isn't always going to avoid you. Younger brains do create new neurons and axon pathways easier than adult brains; however, adults are sincerely as able to discovering success.

nine.Interference is going to keep away from your abilities to use plasticity, this is why all mind of neuroplasticity are tied together.

10. Transference is a response to teach similar behaviors. For instance, it is feasible to use typing to decorate spelling talents.

Now understand that the ones requirements may be utilized in numerous numerous strategies which include assisting with aphasia. Typically, while there is thoughts damage, a person is the use of a device to help known as a speech-producing device or speech-language pathologist, as regards to symptoms like aphasia.

Even even though, the numerous examples provided above cope with speech treatment and brain harm, you may however put into effect the techniques to assist manual you inside the course of better self-motivation. Your achievement will be depending on how willing you are to have a look at the necessities and whether or not or no longer you are working at the areas of the mind at an appropriate time of day to do you any specific.

A paper through the NCBI or National Center for Biotechnology Information has assessed Neuroscience close to boom mindset and intrinsic motivation. There are correlations with how active a mind is and how nicely you may exchange your mind-set and use intrinsic motivators to feature at a higher diploma.

We recognize from the studies that dopamine, which clearly takes place inside the body, allows the thoughts to characteristic at a higher diploma. Dopamine is associated with the reward device, in which our thoughts sends a sign to launch "high-quality feelings" and praise conduct. For Pavlov's canine, it changed into all about saliva being released in anticipation of a praise for meals. Humans react higher while there is a praise. When you combine rewards with new neural pathways, it's miles viable in an effort to alter your perception technique for the higher.

## Chapter 3: Psychology and the Brain

Cognitive psychologists have a test how we accumulate, apprehend, procedure, and keep facts. Using some of the identical machines in remedy, similar to the MRI (magnetic resonance imaging) cognitive psychologists take a look at how the mind reacts to stimulus, collectively with new facts. Through every remedy and psychology, we're able to see what regions of the mind are impacted even as gaining information of recent statistics even as adapting our mind-set, or maybe gaining intrinsic motivation.

The studies have helped us to advantage non-public boom, which includes more self belief and motivation. We also recognize a chunk greater approximately the mind, the way it capabilities and why or while it is able to create new neural pathways for better responses.

In the past we did not understand the connection among psychology and treatment, and consequently, we did no longer be aware of intellectual fitness and handiest involved approximately our physical health. We recognize extra in recent times, which embody the need to make sure intellectual fitness is being assessed and checked for improved normal average overall performance.

It is also approximately the praise device, which Pavlov proved over a century in the beyond. Our intellectual health, the vicinity of emotions, in which we've got extremely good emotions, likes rewards. Our thoughts tells us to never do a little component yet again even as ache, bodily or intellectual takes vicinity. We are not going to intentionally positioned our finger on a warmness variety, as speedy as we learn that it hurts. However, if we praise ourselves thru being lazy in choice to following thru with dreams, it is going to be tougher for us to advantage motivation.

Based on the concept that we will praise ourselves instead of inflicting pain, we want to assess how we are able to use psychology and the mind to acquire a modern-day-day pathway of fulfillment that guarantees we are happier and complete of greater self perception than within the past. Going ahead you may discover ways to use psychology and technological recognize-the way to enhance.

Psychology and Self-Motivation

According to psychologists, there are three factors to motivation:

1.Activation

2.Persistence

3.Intensity

Maslow, a psychologist, said there may be a hierarchy of dreams, which guarantees we encourage for our survival. When we enjoy our survival is in jeopardy we can be activated to behave, we are able to then persist to ensure we live, and relying on the extent of "worry" behind survival we may be exceptionally intense to make sure we stay on.

Skinner believed in reinforcement, similar to Pavlov and his dog, Skinner analyzed people to appearance how advocated reinforcement of particular necessities might probably art work. For instance, is someone greater prompted to succeed whilst effective or horrific reinforcement is provided? The putting cease end result is that with the right degree of terrible reinforcement, a few human beings are much more likely to attain success than if they may be given remarkable reinforcement.

Unfortunately, we will be inclined to be terrible as humans. We live longer on the negatives that display up in our existence and use them to push us to keep away from the horrible situation again.

There are simply as many folks that may be a success primarily based completely mostly on McClelland's achievement precept, which states excellent reinforcement, with set goals is in all likelihood to push someone to have greater motivation. In the administrative center, rewards collectively with a touch plaque or employee of the month can be particularly motivating for certain personalities. They try to do higher for the rewards supplied. For instance, let's consider a plaque is provided for worker of the month, however with that comes a present card or a better parking area. Now greater human beings are stimulated to get the secondary advantage in desire to actually doing a proper venture.

Motivation and the Brain

Science tells us the region of the mind presenting dopamine is wherein we are able to advantage our motivation. Dopamine is an indication made via the usage of using the mind, in which one neuron will pass a sign to a few different to tell your body to launch dopamine. Dopamine while regarding motivation originates from the mesolimbic pathway, which is determined in the center of the mind, in which branches will attain out to locations just like the cortex. The technological understanding isn't always as critical due to the fact the reality that motivation is tied to your cortex, the principle a part of the brain's laptop, and while the proper indicators are launched, your body gets the chemical, and you're rewarded via a experience to collect a few issue or avoid some thing awful. Dopamine is likewise the chemical launched in our fight or flight reaction. For squaddies in struggle, dopamine allows someone react to keep themselves and others from the risk.

When it is associated with motivation to help you become happier, it is approximately the encouragement to act as a way to benefit something actual in choice to to keep away from the horrific. In a test with the aid of Vanderbilt scientists it turned into determined that the ones who've excessive-overall performance degrees have more dopamine of their prefrontal cortex and striatum, in which motivation and reward stand up. Those who slack off have dopamine levels within the anterior insula or a place wherein emotion and chance notion occur.

The vital component is you can tell your frame to offer greater dopamine. You ought to make your mind work with a view to provide bursts of motivation, however it's going to take setting dreams. These goals need to be incremental in nature, so you are building small accomplishments and therefore getting extra dopamine to release in the satisfactory area of the thoughts.

Now which you have an information of ways psychology, the brain, and motivation join, it is time to begin jogging on approaches you can advantage greater motivation and self belief.

The Relationship among Confidence and Motivation

In preceding sections we alluded to the connection amongst self perception and motivation—the need to have every—to absolutely accomplish your purpose of turning into extra endorsed and self guarantee in any scenario.

Motivation is wanted to act. However, it's far your self guarantee which could each assist or save you you inside the ones responsibilities. A individual who views their global in a terrible way has a tendency to lack self notion and be packed with tension. Anxiety may be a motivating trouble or save you your moves. When fear is absolutely too amazing, you fall returned on state of no activity.

Let's study social anxiety for a moment. A person with social tension will refuse to region themselves in social conditions. A companion may also additionally preference to go to a celebration, but the man or woman with social tension will try and find dozens of excuses not to transport. The fear is extra than the praise on this form of scenario.

Another instance approximately self guarantee and motivation can be circle of relatives. We will say a extra more youthful individual, who has a bachelor's degree is disrespected for their profession choice. It is a profession preference that calls for an entire lot of hard paintings, but the economic benefit is pretty small. An aunt is extraordinarily disrespectful in the direction of a more youthful person. She feels the younger character is nugatory, is setting stress on the mother and father, and regularly on the same time because the character tries to talk, the aunt interrupts her, showing derision for her intelligence. Such moves eat away on the self assurance of the character, melancholy devices in, and the younger person well-knownshows it tougher and extra difficult to be stimulated believing the mother and father feel the same manner due to the fact the aunt.

A cycle of loss of ability starts offevolved offevolved, final contact of desires or maybe placing desires becomes reduced. Instead of running, the man or woman attempts to find out topics that bring happiness. It way turning to rewards, without getting the paintings or cause completed. Since it feels higher to examine shows that make the person laugh, this cycle continues, and laziness gadgets in, which creates a cycle of low self-self belief and tension that keeps to prevent motivation.

While the above instance is a terrible statement, self perception and motivation can paintings hand in hand for high quality outcomes. Anxiety can either end up a force of motivation or be decreased to make sure motivation happens. When the stableness of extremely good emotions, self assurance, and anxiety takes location, motivation will growth so that in any situation someone will show super capabilities. A cycle of positives for motivation and self-self warranty in the end cause happiness.

Going ahead strategies to construct motivation and self belief may be furnished. You can take those schooling and wearing sports activities to advantage new heights in artwork, lifestyles, and relationships.

## Chapter 4: Goal Setting

The learning way will in no way save you, however we're finished with the clinical and highbrow speak. It is time so you can advantage a few applicable ideas to help you paintings on yourself-motivation. The key elements to undergo in mind going in advance are:

● Self-motivation is tied to self-self belief and tension.

It is a cyclical dating, that allows you to paintings on one, you want to paintings on the possibility . You are going to advantage facts on a manner to reduce your anxiety to a probable degree that permits you turn out to be more powerful. You also are going to discover recommendations at the way to increase your self-self guarantee.

Goal putting is step one to gaining greater motivation via the use of anxiety and self belief. You need wants to accomplish to have motivation. The drawback to purpose setting is we frequently try to acquire desires which can be beyond our current-day capabilities or desire.

There is a difference amongst a sensible aim and a dream. A dream is a few thing we usually have a tendency to romanticize because the "quality" purpose, however we lack the choice to conform with via and gain it. For instance, you may have changed majors. You concept about the specific maximum crucial, what lifestyles is probably want to have that career, but the reality become truely one-of-a-type. The learning required to obtain the degree and benefit a profession confirmed the fact and your belief were separate. It does no longer advocate you cannot gather a dream, it definitely manner that your beauty of the truth in preference to the "dream" wonderful desires to appear earlier than you can meet that goal.

So, as you start to keep in mind the dreams you want to have, you want to don't forget the truth of the situation.

Another accurate example is of a person who is substantially considering going decrease back to highschool to gain, at least, a cybersecurity certification. The person have become considering beginning this method right away, however then fact sunk in. The man or woman holds  jobs, works six days according to week, is attempting to construct a house and is currently living in flux among houses. Multiple pets and circle of relatives furthermore depend on this individual to assist useful resource them, to clean house, to scrub dishes and apparel, and make meals. The house building goes to be completed via this character and the circle of relatives, in choice to hiring a contractor. Time, this is already an hassle, is quick to become extra restrained. The reality is that taking one or two schooling each eight weeks is not feasible except the man or woman does no longer want to sleep and desires to open up the capability for failure.

It is higher to wait in this form of reason until the person has a slightly less disturbing life.

Say, while the residence is constructed and expenses are fewer, and consequently the removal of the quantity of walking hours is tons much less.

With the examples, you could see why it's miles critical to assess your purpose placing with a hyper-rational thoughts and much less romanticism.

Making a List

1.Get out a chunk of paper or open a phrase processor on your computer.

2.List the assets you need to do. It can encompass profession, courting and one-of-a-kind private dreams, inclusive of touring, getting to know a brand new hobby, and some element else. Your list can also need to embody taking an hour to smooth the house. It is as plenty as you.

three.Beside each aim, if you have now not finished so, write how prolonged it would take to reap the intention in a "nice" situation. For instance, permit's say you need to tour to Japan. A flight is $2,000 out of your area, a week live at a lodge is $2,000, food might be $500, and leisure is $1,000. You want $5,500. Due in your bills, you've got $three hundred left over each month. How many months would not it take to manipulate to pay for $five,500? It will be a touch over a 12 months and a 1/2 of.

You can do the identical for going decrease once more to school and undertaking your career goals. You can also have a software that takes 24 weeks, for $6,000, however have to you do this system as it's far designed, or will you want double the time?

four.You will start taking walks on the fast-time period goals first. Let's say you need to smooth your house. It will take an hour. Get up now and reap this intention. You can come decrease again to the e-book whilst you are performed. In reality, any quick-time period motive you wrote down that may be finished right now—bypass do it.

How do you experience with a goal finished? Do you revel in the pressure is decreased? Do you want to look what you could do next and eliminate from your listing? Most people do— it is the mixture of dopamine and praise that brings your choice higher.

You aren't going to set a date completion for the opportunity goals. Being too unique to your purpose placing can motive faulty initiation, pressure, and heightened anxiety. If you positioned a cause that is a year down the road, an emergency takes region, and you need to increase the of completion date, you could lose self belief. We will now not set you up for this form of "failure." Rather, you will study your goals, the capability quantity of time for final touch, and determine preference reason you will deal with next.

To help collect your motivation, self belief, and decrease tension, you need to pick out small dreams on the start and art work as a good deal as the greater complicated desires.

What is a few aspect for your motive listing or you could located to your reason listing to complete day after today? Write it down and popularity on that aim.

Each time you fulfill a motive, mark it off the listing or create a listing of finished desires. It is as a good deal as you and your wants to decide if you need a present day listing or to absolutely bypass something off.

Some of the easy desires also can moreover seem and reappear on the listing, given you need to smooth your home often it is a every day, weekly, or month-to-month goal to meet. But, the act of getting this mission completed is in which the confidence boom will derive from and assist you meet one-of-a-kind goals.

The prolonged-time period desires that require coins are every now and then wherein a person can falter drastically within the motivation branch. We will popularity on the Japan instance. You apprehend in 18 months costs for a flight, inn, and specific holiday prices can growth or lower based totally on the recognition of the destination. You may additionally additionally furthermore save $5,500 and find out you need $8,000 in 18 months. It is straightforward to expect your intention putting has failed or that you are by no means going as a manner to have enough money the holiday.

Neuroplasticity is needed in this case. It is time to retrain your thoughts. Rather than questioning a few aspect is "by no means" going to seem, you need to hobby on the reason you attained. You met the purpose through saving $5,500. Changes in price are from your manipulate.

You can decide to make certain the trade in rate that could arise in 18 months does no longer have an impact to your real reason. For financially responsible humans, it's far possible to use a credit score score card. You positioned the vacation in your card, you located the card within the secure, and you are making monthly bills of $three hundred.

At the give up of 18 months, the card is paid off, assuming you paid no hobby.

The instance is why you need to evaluate your desires with a hyper-rational thoughts. For people who are surprising with the term it implies that you set dreams with out emotion, you step lower returned and examine the capability failure factors, the reality of gaining the purpose, and what you can do to make certain you whole the aim.

The holiday to Japan showed you can pay for the vacation with a credit card to get the first-rate cost. The disadvantage is you may have an emergency at the same time as you need the $three hundred for something greater critical than the credit rating card rate. What ought to you do to account for this case? Would it purpose you to move off track and quality make the minimal fee to the cardboard? Is it certainly nicely well worth being in debt to meet the purpose information that existence can throw matters at you which ones of them might be out of your manage?

You want to evaluate the anxiety this kind of situation may cause. Would this tension decorate or lower your motivation? If it'd decrease your motivation, you can't pay for a intention with a credit rating card.

Enough on this situation, allow's not bore you. Just recall it as you create your purpose listing.

Concentrate on the subsequent:

● The aim

● The time it might take to finish the purpose

● Any sudden complications you could recall, which incorporates an emergency, infection, hobby loss, or other problem

● Your tension stage about the purpose and what should reduce the tension or push you to be prompted

If you could maintain the four elements above in your mind while placing goals, you're lots a lot much less apt to set desires  you can not accomplish, and be  via lower self perception, and for that reason "failure" and stepped forward tension.

With goals in thoughts, we are capable of flow to the next degree in motivation and self perception building.

# Chapter 5: Decluttering Every Aspect of Life

"Decluttering" is a term being carried out in some of strategies, together with reducing relationships, distractions, and cleaning. Originally, the time period became coined for a minimalist way of life wherein people are looking for to appearance fewer devices round the house that acquire dirt and reason tension.

We have taken the term and done it to more areas of our lives to gain greater happiness in lifestyles, art work, and relationships.

It is a concept that allows you to assist growth self belief and growth self-motivation.

Physical Clutter

Physical litter refers to materialistic requirements. Look across the room you're in, what do you spot? As you observe the room, are there matters you have not looked at for 6 months? Are there things you located on a desk for comfort in desire to necessity?

As an example, allow's say our busy man or woman who cannot take cybersecurity guides, lives in a small place. Due to the industrial enterprise in life, mail is on a couple of surfaces, journals are everywhere, books are stacked everywhere in the place, and dust bunnies are extra partners to the pets.

How do you found the individual might probable enjoy getting into the house, going to the workspace, and seeing subjects everywhere, with out a smooth company, sample, or empty floor?

Each individual is unique, however it's miles extra apt to mention the man or woman ought to discover it hard to compartmentalize. The litter pushes the tension to increase, so the individual begins considering all the obligations that need to be completed, the circle of relatives drama that is taking money and time some distance from precise goals, and now the inducement to get work performed is at an all time low. The person desires to tackle all desires, but the

47

stress and tension to do the most essential work first, what makes the coins, will growth. This boom in pressure and anxiety reduces the motivation, the character desires to are searching out some thing to persuade them to glad or as a minimum revel in an awful lot a whole lot less worn-out and to trust the thoughts has the energy to ensure the final touch of the most important goal.

If the man or woman alternatively took ten mins an afternoon to place topics of their vicinity, put off the useless mail, and prepare items used each day, the workspace can be clean, decluttered, useable, and the motivation may be there to finish the mission with out anxiety developing. The interest could be at the essential aim and now not on everything else that desires to be completed but isn't always getting finished.

From the instance, you may see the cyclical problems that physical clutter may also moreover need to create, relying on your personality. Some people have the ability to stay in a massive huge range and by no means see it. It have to sincerely create extra anxiety to lessen the clutter than to leave it.

What form of individual are you? If you believe you could deal with bodily litter, yet by no means seem to have motivation it's time to alternate.

Some humans can leave litter, ignoring the mess, because their laser consciousness is on one motive, but the key is the man or woman has the incentive to complete the art work and is doing so, regardless of the arena round them.

There are little topics that can be accomplished to disregard or to lessen the clutter.

Ignore the Clutter for Motivation

Let's say you are the first example, in which the litter is bothering you, but you do now not have time to fix it due to the fact the intention is sincerely too crucial. You do now not need to lose to your self and desire to advantage motivation.

1.Create tunnel imaginative and prescient. If you've got got a blouse with a hood, put on it and located the hood up, blocking off your peripheral vision.

2.Move matters closer that you'll be looking on the same time as completing the venture, along with a tumbler of water near and within your imaginative and prescient for easy obtain.

three.If you are the use of a laptop, but time is increasing tension, cover the clock.

four.Take a deep breath and permit it out.

five.Turn on relaxing music, if possible, inclusive of latest age or classical. Something that instills a snug thoughts, and no longer some thing as a way to cause your coronary coronary heart to race.

6.Focus exceptional on what's in the front of you that topics to finish the mission.

7.When you've got were given completed 1 / four of the undertaking, upward push up, dispose of some aspect from the paintings region that creates clutter. Put it a few other vicinity, location it in which it belongs, or throw the trash away.

8.Go once more on your assignment, along side your tunnel imaginative and prescient.

Keep to the ones steps until the mission is complete. Set small wants to satisfy at a few stage within the important task. For example, in case you recognize a assignment must take you 5 hours, and you could want lunch in the middle of it, then set a motive to satisfy earlier than the meal, and praise yourself with lunch.

Let's say you want to kind up a document this is 10,000 words, and you could type 2,000 phrases in an hour. By midday, you want to have five,000 words entire, and therefore you've got got half of the document for after your meal.

You received a harm, meals to maintain you going, and also you finished a intention, that could help reduce the anxiety of assembly the closing date through manner of the stop of the day.

In this type of scenario, you could set sixty seconds apart every hour to arise, stretch, and sit down down down go into reverse to help preserve your body active. Studies show if you have been sitting you want to stand to help convey lower once more strength.

Reduce the Clutter

You have one tactic for coping with physical litter that may be impacting your motivation and anxiety. Let's recollect a tremendous alternative. You may additionally find out that till you lessen the muddle you are not capable of attention on the crucial venture. Yes, you could want to attack the complete problem, however for now, to reduce the muddle to your art work place (going with the paintings instance) is crucial.

1.Clean up your artwork floor.

2.Start with the mail, throw away the envelopes, and placed the payments or paperwork in a place that is supposed for such topics. You may want to probably placed the whole thing in the respective folders or in a stack at the nook of your table.

3.Work through the regions which may be bothering you, together with placing books near the cabinets in which they flow into.

four.Once the floor is clean, and your imaginative and prescient sees cleanliness, wipe the floor of dirt, particles, or doggy hair.

5.Now, you've got were given executed a cause.

6.Use this very last contact and the feelings it furnished to start the critical task.

You benefit greater attention on this method than you will possibly with tunnel imaginative and prescient, which ultimately saves you time. If you constantly see the mess and cannot forget about it, your thoughts are at the clutter, this means that that that you are lowering your interest on the reason and making sure it takes you longer—probably beyond remaining date—to satisfy the reason.

Decide what type of character you've got got regarding tunnel imaginative and prescient or clutter good buy. Use the approach that fits you pleasant to artwork on decluttering your bodily floor.

The key thing is to comprehend that small desires eventually of the method are going to offer you with a enjoy of fulfillment and happiness, to be able to increase your regular motivation.

The smooth act of starting and completing a simple task makes you need to see what else you could do. It is the dopamine that ensures your desire to live on task is there.

Obviously, the instance is extra about a bit scenario, where physical clutter creates distractions and anxiety. You may moreover have a lifestyles that lets in you loads of time to carry out every day exercise exercises, which consist of cleaning, but you continuously keep away from it due to the fact there is not anything to push you.

Eliminating Clutter whilst Motivation is a Factor

You are someone with masses of time and you suspect to yourself "Oh, I'll do this the next day." Then you discover some element to distract you. Perhaps, your emotional usa is precarious because of life struggles primary to anxiety and despair, consequently, you're asking what the issue of doing something is. For the anxiety and depression, looking for help is essential. When you're a person distracted by the usage of the usage of a laugh and amusement rather than timing troubles or emotional pressure, the following recommendations may additionally assist.

1.Set a goal, including ten minutes spent on decluttering and cleansing.

2.Turn on the right track, TV you may concentrate to inside the heritage or ask someone to time you.

3.Being the project.

Studies show that when you start a few element, irrespective of a time purpose in thoughts, you may need to complete the mission. Now, understand it will no longer art work for every body. A person with ADHD can begin a cause and go away it unfulfilled through manner of way of having distracted about some component else.

You should recognize your person in advance than you could observe pointers that come up with the results you want.

It is even higher whilst you recognize you have got set a time restriction and completed the challenge earlier than the limit befell. For example, a person could in all likelihood have set a goal of venture half the word remember with the useful resource of midday, and found they did greater than that, they passed it with the useful aid of one hundred phrases, in advance than eleven:fifty 5 am.

The issue is you want to recognize who you're, your strengths and limitations, and the rewards so that it will make you smile. Once you have the ones elements, you'll start developing new pathways to make certain motivation lets in you entire any challenge you positioned your thoughts to and therefore you will take on opportunities that end up available.

Emotional Clutter

Reducing physical muddle is regularly less complicated than handling emotional baggage on the assignment of having inspired. But there are topics you could do to help alleviate a number of your issues to assist deliver lower returned your motivation.

●   Eliminate any possible illnesses, illnesses, or troubles that might have an effect in your motivation. Depression maintains being noted as it does have an massive effect in your capability to complete obligations. Depression is associated with hormonal imbalances, so it is able to be associated with ailments or issues like hyper or hypothyroid. Other hormones if now not furnished enough can mimic depression. Depression is one clinical and highbrow scenario that may be addressed with remedy.

● Anxiety is every distinct psychological hassle that can relate to contamination, as an entire lot because it relates to at least one's highbrow health. Fear may be a steady companion or situational. It is feasible you could take remedy for the tension if it is a everyday associate. There are other techniques consisting of meditation and breathing techniques you can use to reduce anxiety at the identical time as it's miles at its height.

The terrific things to do close to emotional muddle is to address matters head-on. Do not allow them to boom and end up more difficult. Working through the topics that have an impact on you the most is critical. But, no longer commonly viable. For instance, someone must have such plenty of topics happening from an excessive amount of paintings, too little cash, housing worries, little one care issues, and quite a bit else that focusing at the maximum crucial challenge because of the fact tough. Instead of putting apart the matters that aren't as essential, you will probable keep to reflect onconsideration on the whole lot  and enjoy like your thoughts is going to blow up.

The suitable information—it gained't—you may moreover broaden compartmentalization. Creating a subject for storing the subjects you're no longer capable of consider right now is not confined to men. Somewhere alongside the road ladies have been instructed that we couldn't in all likelihood compartmentalize the severa responsibilities in our thoughts and consciousness on simply one aspect. However, billions of girls do that every day. We truely choose to speak about our emotions and show our affections more conveniently than guys do.

How Compartmentalization Works

1.Picture a subject in your thoughts.

2.Place the numerous mind you have inner, developing a contemporary area for every exquisite concept. For instance, emotions have an area, anxiety has some different, private responsibilities, and expert dreams every have their very own spot.

three.Leave simplest the maximum essential venture out and within the major edge of your thoughts. Concentrate on the stairs that want to be finished.

4.You can mentally lock the container in case you preference. You also can pressure it closed whilst your mind starts offevolved thinking about subjects that are not the precept scenario. Visualization is high-quality for this kind of approach due to the reality you may mentally remember all of these thoughts being securely placed from your instantaneous hobby and awareness on what topics.

five.When one mission is complete, you can take out some distinct from the box and recognition on it.

6.Sometimes you could go away mind locked within the field for several days or perhaps weeks, till you're capable of ultimately face them or deal with them, alongside aspect emotional turmoil that reasons undue strain or ache.

You will want to cope with the emotional luggage finally. However, compartmentalization is one manner to area it at the over again-burner till you've got the time or are equipped. There also are steps you may use to simply "permit things pass." Negative emotions aren't essential to hold around. Realizing what you can control and trade in preference to what you can't is a way to allow pass of the terrible and recognition on the positives. We can't manage special humans, their mind, emotions, or movements. To declutter your thoughts similarly, from time to time it's far vital to absolutely and actively country what is real— you are your very very very own electricity, your mind is able to reading new subjects, and absolutely every body who attempts to eat away at your self belief and motivation is not well truely well worth taking note of or being round.

There are times when you need to walk a long way from family, pals, or buddies because of the reality you recognise they are permitting you to lose your motivation or self belief. Unhappy people can supply you down and they're able to distract you because they're in search of to advantage your interest, diverting it from what subjects.

As we paintings through new sections on motivation, self assure, and anxiety, we are able to have a look at relationships. More information about how relationships with buddies, own family, and pals can effect your motivation is probably discussed. For now, maintain in thoughts your emotional united states of america.

Do you revel in at peace? Is your mind going a mile a minute with too many thoughts? Are your thoughts stopping you from taking motion on something due to the reality there may be too much taking region or are you looking to distract your self with rewards earlier than you complete the art work?

It is a cycle we will get into, in which the rewards show up in advance than we're carried out, and it's miles tough to break. Luckily, your neuroplasticity makes it feasible to redirect your brain to triumph over the awful cycles you is probably in and advantage the private increase you choice.

## Chapter 6: Discovering Who You Are

Motivation comes from self assure, however how do we broaden self perception and maintain it as adults? What if we've got were given someone who constantly tells us how disenchanted they'll be in us, how worthless we are or exclusive horrible things? It is hard to assemble self assurance let alone keep it in adulthood.

People who've masses of self assurance understand this is comes from inner, honestly as a good deal because it comes from awesome people and events. The secret is to discover who you're without the influences of others. Many might speak over with this as unbiased strength. Some are born with the innate capacity to be strong with out the have an effect on of others.

It is difficult for the ones people to anticipate what it is probably want to not have the inner energy to be impartial on what others reflect onconsideration on them.

What someone with self assurance and internal energy might probable inform you— is you want to recognize who you're and be comfortable along with your strengths and barriers.

An instance of someone who can conquer: a more youthful girl become the 5th to be born, in a own family of 5 daughters, fashionable. She come to be not taught to prepare dinner. She modified into advised she changed into too silly to do anything but reduce hair. Her best choice for after excessive university changed into to go to splendor school and turn out to be a cosmetologist. Her complete life she concerned approximately coins due to the fact her dad and mom did now not have an awful lot. With a lack of self notion, but a type heart, this individual have come to be a cosmetologist, joined her husband in manufacturing, labored retail, and finally went to university to end up a licensed nursing assistant and treatment beneficial useful resource.

At instances she even though lacks self belief and panics at the same time as there isn't always sufficient coins. However, through locating someone who treated her as an same, who informed her she didn't want his permission to take commands or have a laugh, she have emerge as capable of obtain new heights and be comfortable with who she is as a mother, accomplice, and individual.

You have the capability to use your mind to rewrite the way you consider your self. Furthermore, you may artwork in yourself assure and start ignoring the internal and outer voices that damage your motivation and factor of view. Figuring Out Who You Are

It is not a laugh to take the gloves off and throw down, adequate, so enough of the boxing metaphors which can be better proper for men! The element is you want to investigate yourself in an impartial way, that is one of the hardest things you can ever do.

1.Have you ever lived by myself?

2.Have you lived greater than 1,000 miles out of your mother and father?

three.Was there a time you knew you can call your mother and father, however they might be no longer able to help you, without delay or in any respect?

four.Do you view your self in remarkable or negative terms?

5.Do you consider you studied you don't have any disturbing or proscribing developments?

6.Have you ever been fired?

7.Have you ever been rewarded at artwork?

8.How lengthy do you maintain jobs?

nine.How regularly do you communicate in your friends?

10. Do you enjoy uncomfortable in case you are on my own for a few hours or worse numerous days?

eleven. Do you go out extra than you stay home to keep away from handling loneliness or being alone?

The questions should pass on. The trouble is to use these eleven questions to start the self-mirrored photo. You need to be honest. If you can't consider the answers, consider finding an internet man or woman check to help you discover your non-public attributes and wherein you may fall short.

For example, a person finds many humans at paintings regard her to be fantastic with cash and the arithmetic it includes. But the person thinks the other with reference to math. Yes, on the same time as counting and reconciling coins she is succesful; but, counting again alternate the use of the antique university technique is hard. She considers it to be just as difficult as algebra and calculus with all of the ones useless $x + y =$? She is likewise conscious that her introversion and social anxiety make it more difficult for her to narrate to clients.

Our instance is what you want to advantage even as you observe your self—the potential to virtually accept any limitations you have got—to upward push to the demanding conditions. Mistakes happen, this is some different lesson to have a look at. The same individual with the resource of twist of fate mischarged a patron, charging too little and had to name the man or woman to rate the perfect amount. It might have been a devastating state of affairs, riddled with guilt and horrible thoughts, but the character assessed how often this sort of mistake had took place to her. It in no way had in advance than. In twenty plus years of running retail, she had in no way charged a customer too little or too much.

The lesson in this phase in case you are the only who involves a desire what you decided and revel in; therefore, you are the only person who can in reality check who you are with effective thoughts. Seeking an unbiased, independent opinion can be beneficial, especially, if you find out you struggle to analyze yourself in an independent way.

But, try it first. List your attributes. List the belongings you experience you may do higher. Consider what you've got got attempted, but decided no achievement with, which incorporates a few factor you love, but don't have the abilities to healthy professionals.

As an example, a pastry chef bakes awesome pies, however a home pie is probably sloppy with the crust, the apples or blueberries might be a runny, however as a minimum it tastes fantastic regardless of the interesting presentation. Another person can also stitch amazingly however lack the functionality to go away their feelings at domestic.

Hundreds of examples may be used to speak approximately a way to observe yourself in comparison to others as a way to discover your strengths or weaknesses. It is an area to begin and now not supposed to be the complete approach.

The idea is to get to a degree wherein you could admit you are not as first rate at a few aspect as you would like to be or as someone else, and it's miles adequate because of the fact you are having a laugh while you're doing the undertaking.

Unbiased Opinions

Not every body can step yet again and be hyper-rational when they decide who they may be. One's upbringing can decide your talents to do that kind of issue. You can train your self to do this even though.

● Think approximately a awesome or impediment you have got had been given.

● Why do you discovered it's miles a extraordinary or bad?

● From your upbringing, what can also effect your factor of view?

● What academic know-how is probably affecting the way you recognize topics?

● What influences might probable pop out of your dad and mom in place of friends you have got were given met?

● Take someone from TV, a ebook, or movie and examine the character. What perceptions do you have got, how do you relate, now take a look at online, and look at what the author says approximately the character or what different evaluations exist. Are there topics on your assessment that healthy and others that don't, in which you would possibly have a one of a kind opinion due to upbringing or cultural assumptions primarily based totally on in that you live?

These are just a few of the techniques you may use to assist advantage a modern mindset and find out how your mind and movements might also create a biased opinion until you decide wherein they may be coming from. Some human beings are definitely better at searching at reviews and assessing why anyone has the views they do, and wherein the fact is.

These strategies are going that will help you discover self guarantee and motivation because of the truth they'll be forcing you to assess your perceptions and the regions of your lifestyles in that you started out to lose self notion or motivation, and now you may paintings in the path of correcting it. They don't work for all people however have been quite a success for parents which are open to exploring who they're and studying a way to grow to be extra confident and stimulated.

## Chapter 7: Mindset Changes

Neuroplasticity is the very idea of thoughts-set modifications. You understand the era in the back of the techniques, now it is time to help your mind shape new pathways for better thinking strategies.

Willpower is an critical component as regards to changing to be higher triggered and assured. In reality, we need to in all likelihood list some of words that might be beneficial, but what you want are strategies.

You need to begin slow with motivation, anxiety, and self guarantee. If you rush into matters too rapid, you'll maintain to fall again into vintage styles. One of the interesting elements approximately our mind-set and the usage of neuroplasticity thoughts is you could awaken in some unspecified time in the future with new bodily sports, and never leave out the antique ones.

It does now not arise in a single day, as an opportunity it takes place frequently until you test yourself inside the reflect and apprehend you've got got made amazing modifications to your existence. It may not assist to look at this sort of declaration, but the truth is frequently plenty plenty much less complex than we make it.

Mindset Exercise 1:

1.Start with a small intention.

2.The goal may be some thing from ten mins of cleaning or ingesting higher.

three.Outline the reason or motives why you preference to make the mindset trade.

Motivation comes from wishing to remedy a aim. To end up extra prompted, you need to fulfill these dreams, and you want to pick out something that you like to do. Obviously, life is not truthful, it brings on topics we don't want to face or obligations we don't like doing, collectively with laundry and cleaning.

But, it is also the small goals which can push us to emerge as greater triggered within the subjects we honestly need.

For instance, you'll probably set a goal of studying one e-book a month. You love analyzing, however you in no manner seem to have time for it. By placing a purpose, you're greater apt to try to make that reason than no longer.

four.Publish your aim. Social media makes it easier on the way to keep on your dreams. Even for folks who are not as social, publishing desires on-line makes positive that a person available may additionally keep you responsible. Will they? Maybe no longer. But, a slight worry or trouble of embarrassment makes you agree with you studied they could.

You don't should use social media to put up your dreams. Some goals you have is probably too embarrassing to percentage with the arena, alongside side weight loss. There are useful resource businesses, circle of relatives, and pals who can help with the greater non-public desires. You also can art work as a awesome deal as those dreams.

For the start of the thoughts-set adjustments a good way to supply you more motivation, the focus is going to be on a mission you could consequences give up and experience true about.

Cleaning is an easy cause to talk approximately for motivation, generally due to the truth no character loves to easy or those who do discover they don't have enough time to preserve up with cleaning as they would like.

Let's say you area the motive as cleaning.

You intend on cleansing one room in your own home in the subsequent 30 minutes.

Why—you have selected a room that is bothering you, including distracting you from the artwork you want to do—the workplace.

You want a person to preserve you accountable as a motivational trouble. You inform your companion, widespread exclusive, or anybody else what you may do.

five.Offer yourself an incentive.

An incentive or reward goes that will help you look at via, even greater than telling someone what your motive is. The praise have to be a few aspect appropriate for the task accessible.

Cleaning is a want that we typically need extra motivation to devote, consequently, the praise need to be some component that will help you retrain your thoughts and trade your thoughts-set about cleansing.

A praise does not have to be meals, drink, or a address. Rather, the incentive to complete the challenge need to be a few component associated with the room. It need to pass again to the why.

As you speak yourself into cleaning the room, similar to the place of job, tell yourself the why—you'll be capable of pay interest, you may get extra carried out, you could find out some thing you really want for each other task. We want to keep going, but you get the element. The why and the reward are similar.

Since you're still starting out and you may have motivational issues approximately without a doubt changing your thoughts's neural pathways, you may make the first reward a piece higher. Perhaps, this primary time, you consume a chunk of chocolate.

Here's the way to make the "brilliant" praise a few component you want to paintings hard for:

● Make the praise some issue you do no longer have in the residence, however choice.

If you've got got chocolate inside the residence, then make it a dessert you not often have or some problem else you recall worthwhile. In this primary assignment, you are showing your mind why you want to entire the challenge.

Now, all of us apprehend the motive worthwhile your self every time can lead to problem. Your thoughts starts offevolved to

79

say, "Oh, bypass the project and reward yourself now." You are not able to reward your mind the subsequent time with a few detail higher than asking "why."

Your intention with the primary reason you whole is to ensure the neural pathway goes to form for additonal motivation. The subsequent time you complete a purpose, phrases want to have greater energy.

You need to obtain the point in that you are satisfied to tell yourself what a outstanding activity you have got got finished and how proud you're. Unfortunately, it does take time to make in reality "terms" your motivator.

It is also essential to factor out that every so often you need more help for obligations. The cause you want to continuously inform a person your purpose, even a stupid, small aim is to make certain someone is going to preserve you responsible. The disadvantage with relying on someone else is they can allow you.

You want to choose out a person who is drastically influenced and could apprehend why you experience the want to benefit extra motivation.

6.The remaining step for converting your attitude is to copy the reason attainment often. Each mission you need to complete for the day need to be rewarded with incredible mind.

It may be silly to mention a few aspect like, "Great, you obtain away from bed in recent times. Task one complete." However, your thoughts likes paying attention to this. You can continuously exchange the phrase to encompass one of a kind morning obligations, which encompass "oh, I awoke earlier than the alarm." Whatever is new and one among a kind, however makes you experience appropriate approximately your day is some thing you need to spend a few seconds reflecting on due to the reality repetition is fundamental.

Remember those ten standards of neuroplasticity and the way repetition and the use of the equal terms can advantage you? Here is in which they come into play. Each time a intention is met, you operate phrases to reward yourself for the accomplishment, and you retain with this pattern. Soon, you are not going to need to actively consider the goals, the why or the reward, you may simply get the undertaking completed.

Our lives are also now not smooth. We have others who rely upon us or we rely on others. With paintings, existence, and relationships all coalescing taking the time for matters that are not a situation is wherein we have a tendency to lose motivation and but they're the regions that make it greater hard for us to complete the concern responsibilities because of the muddle brought about in the mind.

Everything is a cycle, so if you may educate your mind to really receive the mundane on

the element of dreams you've got were given,
you may end up greater a hit.

# Chapter 8: Work Motivation

Successful freelance employees advantage their success because of the fact they do no longer have problems with motivation. Obviously, skills moreover plays a element, however that is all about motivation, so permit's popularity on freelance personnel.

What do you discovered a freelancer faces every day, once they upward push up, have art work, and stay at home?

They face masses of each day obligations, together with personal and paintings goals. But, how do they stay stimulated once they search around the house understanding matters aren't getting achieved?

It is compartmentalization. Remember the communique above approximately setting matters in a container and best considering them when you have the time? Freelancers are notable at this, further to tunnel vision.

Freelancers address their art work as although they have got a hobby outside of the house. They wake up, put together for the day, review the responsibilities to finish, and wonderful while the art work is finished can they attention on personal ideas.

To do some aspect else have to jeopardize their employment. On days at the same time as there can be no paintings, it's time to get private duties completed. There may be pressure if now not enough paintings is coming in, that can have an effect on motivation, however that is a different situation rely.

When you visit paintings each day, you've got topics that need to be completed. If your paintings ordinary normal overall performance is slow or stricken by motivation, you received't have the project lengthy or you may in no manner get promoted. Employers look for folks that are stimulated, even folks who take the initiative on a venture.

Your very motivation for art work is cash.

● You want profits to preserve your own home, automobile, and to make certain you have got were given meals.

● Most jobs, not all, but many do provide insurance, private days, excursion days, and one-of-a-kind advantages.

The worry of dropping your task; therefore, your advantages and the cash is wherein your motivation for strolling at a respectable degree takes place. Now, it does no longer suggest you have got the inducement to do more than you're asked.

College college students are a wonderful instance. For parents that during no manner had a project, they is probably informed to do a little factor, and do it once, then the boss has to maintain reminding them to do the assignment once more.

Motivating Yourself at Work

It is time for the query and solution length all over again!

1.Are you happy with the amount of pay you earn?

2.Why are you glad or unhappy with it? Look on the cash objectively.

You have to be happy if you make sufficient to pay your bills and spend money on a saving account. You have to be satisfied if you are capable of take a vacation each year, without fear that you could bypass closely into debt. You need to be happy in case you take a look at the corporation you determine in and make a comparative sum of money in keeping with hour or income.

You ought to be sad if any of the above are actual, mainly if everything is authentic.

You should now not be unhappy in case you suppose you deserve greater than you get, but even as assessing your paintings common overall performance in an unbiased way you recognise you can do more to earn your salary.

3.Do you like your hobby?

four.Have you idea approximately a promoting?

5.When it's miles slow at art work, do you look around to find out outstanding responsibilities or do you pop open Netflix and watch a TV show?

In a genuinely ideal international anybody would really like their manner, but they don't. It might be the choice of a function that end up to be had, and a person end up complacent. You also can have worked difficult for the diploma you've got were given got and now you hate it.

Only you could change your employment popularity. If you want seventy five% of your hobby, then you need to take the downsides with the placement. Anything a top notch deal less and you could want to begin looking for a modern-day profession.

It is okay to test out amazing industries. College university college college students are taught to pick out out out a exquisite, follow via, and get a career. A better concept is to test a few jobs, see the fact of the artwork, after which invest in a destiny. It lets in you turn out to be extra stimulated for your career desire.

There is not anything incorrect with switching jobs, so long as you deliver the location time, and you figure towards some component that is going to be better for you and in addition motivating.

One instance is of a woman who had lots of motivation, independence, and tunnel imaginative and prescient while it got here to her diploma. This person worked in creation, clothing retail, hostess, airport retail, financial institution, scuba instructor/lodge supervisor, a movie theater, freelance author, and e-book place supplier. She additionally worked as a barista a couple of times. Over the years, she has determined out that her love of books, tea, and espresso are pointing her towards a profession that might encompass all three. The dream is to very very very own a store internet hosting tea tastings, selling espresso and books. There are elements to the career that aren't superb, inclusive of having the choice for themed tea tastings, but social tension to host them. But the reward outweighs the panic of public speakme.

The point is, if you have a passion for a few issue, which include a hobby, you then truely definitely may in all likelihood consider converting careers as it might surely provide you with more motivation.

If you are unwilling to trade your profession, proper proper right here are a few recommendations.

1.Assess the task.

2.Determine the advantage of the challenge. How will it assist your employers, how have to it assist you, who else might in all likelihood advantage out of your very last touch of the art work?

3.What is a non-public praise you may provide your self? It may be self-pride, a address, or some thing else you discover profitable.

You do no longer need to do a task due to the reality a person else will reward you. If you do a challenge this is a part of your each day hobby, you then definately want to no longer count on someone to praise you for doing what you are purported to do.

But you can begin to search for techniques to get the kudos out of your boss for matters which are above and beyond your art work. The delight of doing extra than you are paid for can help you reach promotions.

Whenever it involves motivation at paintings, constantly keep in mind the venture, the gain of that task for others, and how you could for my part experience particular about its completion. There are mundane topics together with going through a listing of 3,4 hundred books, looking at what number of had been presented within the preceding yr, if the stock is 0, and identifying if the call desires to be deleted. The praise for some element so mundane, knowing the stock is wiped clean up and there can be less confusion approximately what books are in the store or are well-known.

Lastly, motivation is ready satisfaction, even in paintings.

Lost Satisfaction

It is viable you are searching out processes to be extra inspired as a girl because you've got out of area the satisfaction of a project properly carried out. It's smooth while you artwork in someone's global or for male bosses who don't think "kudos" are vital. When you are positioned down or your boss loses their mood inside the direction of you because of the reality they are unhappy, satisfaction on your work surroundings can plummet.

Here is the aspect wherein you need to remember your need for unbiased pride. Many human beings like a person else to offer them nice comments, type words, and to see that they will be doing an awesome undertaking. There is not some thing wrong with having that desire.

But you should no longer get bogged down with the resource of it.

How you positioned of yourself is more crucial than any words from each different individual. If you can whole a task and inform your self you likely did notable, then that is all you need.

1.After each task you complete, tell yourself you probable did properly.

2.Accept that errors display up, and those are not best.

3.If a mistake happens, accept it, have a look at from it, and go along with the glide on—do not live on it.

The above three steps will help you get your paintings pleasure lower back. You also can start to retrain your thoughts so you permit the negatives move. It takes actively wondering to ensure this happens, at least inside the beginning. Once you get used to being satisfied by manner of the small subjects, it'll get less difficult to experience satisfied with yourself and go with the flow on with greater motivation.

## Chapter 9: Personal Motivation

Personal motivation consists of lifestyles and relationship subjects. You must argue that lifestyles is all approximately paintings and relationships, plus time to be on my own. For the benefit of communique and tips, we will use "life" to speak about domestic and one-of-a-kind personal responsibilities that don't involve your relationships or art work.

Getting stimulated for the laundry, grocery shopping for, taking the children spherical city, and plenty of one of a kind subjects are part of non-public motivation. The discussion may be on how you can juggle plenty, experience suitable approximately it, and entire all the obligations.

Think approximately your dad and mom. Did you located they need to be heroes due to the reality they seemed to get the entirety finished or did, they just seem as workaholics? How did that make you revel in? What did you make a decision as you reached maturity, you will do to keep away from the errors your parents made?

Don't worry approximately answering the questions, surely have them inside the decrease once more of your mind. Some mother and father are able to seem like fantastic human beings. They rise up, get the youngsters off the bed, have breakfast geared up, get the packed lunches from the night time time earlier than out of the fridge, force the youngsters to school, select up the children, help with homework, have dinner ready, easy the dishes each night, and % lunches. Oh, and by way of way of the use of the manner, they paintings 8 hours a day too.

The trick is getting help from the partner and the children. Chores are a exceptional lesson because it teaches a toddler, they have to do some thing, even though it's a protracted manner no fun, as it's far part of lifestyles. But not all and sundry has the equal instructions, and occasionally regardless of it, laziness wins in place of motivation.

Getting the Life Tasks Complete

1.Retrain your mind.

2.Life duties ought to be achieved—no one else will do them for you.

3.Establish new each day exercises.

4.Reward your self.

You are going to retrain your thoughts in this motivation lesson. You will hold repeating that the task need to be completed, and no man or woman else goes that will help you. Now, you can have kids and a accomplice, and feel free to enlist their help. But, in case you tell yourself no character is going to assist, then you haven't anybody to depend on.

The feeling of being independent and on my own is a first-rate motivator.

Most of all you need new routines. It can also take reorganizing your lifestyles, in conjunction with your private home. To hold an area a great deal much less cluttered everything need to have its personal area, and also you positioned it in that vicinity every time you return home. What you can do "now" saves you from a build up of obligations for later. It takes five minutes or lots much less to start the laundry, every other 5 to change it to the dryer. Each cycle is ready thirty mins to an hour, in some unspecified time in the future of which generation you could do numerous matters.

If you can method responsibilities in that you apprehend switch tasking, then you could complete pretty a bit in a brief quantity of time.

By coming domestic and setting all the groceries away, you don't ought to do it later. When you come home, you placed your footwear inside the closet, grasp your coat, this keeps matters first rate. The idea is that you may do such subjects with any venture.

Cleaning ten minutes an afternoon, in a one-of-a-kind region, allow's you cycle within the direction of your complete house just so every month it's miles virtually easy. Getting in wearing occasions which incorporates this makes it much less complicated to stay inspired.

Initially, you start with a reward, including a tumbler of wine at the stop of the night time time. After a piece time, you want satisfaction to be the handiest praise you want.

Never fall into the entice of trying satisfaction out of your youngsters or partner. You aren't going to get it as a whole lot as you want it. Just consider decrease decrease lower back to adolescence or maybe recently in adulthood, at the same time as your parent said some element about doing something that benefits all people and you did not famend it or worse, you said a few component like "oh, that is splendid. It desired it."

We are through way of nature lazy, even in our compliments, so if you prevent searching earlier to such matters from others, and only count on them from your self, you will be happier and your motivation for the obligations will growth.

Self-motivation is normally going to be about your dreams and the rewards you supply yourself, no longer what others offer. Relationships and Motivation

Relationships whether or not or not they'll be with kids, parents, buddies, accomplice, or buddies can assist or forestall motivation. There are folks who may be our "inner" voice and others who grow to be our terrible inner voice. We name the horrific instigator an enabler.

An enabler is a person who is going to make it more difficult so as to stay inspired, to stay heading in the right direction along side your dreams, and final make it more tough for you to succeed. Let's bypass all over again to the freelancer.

The freelancer had an enabler in her existence. This individual may additionally want to speak her into going out, they could spend the day shopping for, after which say, "oh properly, you can do the paintings the following day." Now, the detail approximately the artwork is that it would normally are to be had in at some level within the late morning hours, heaps later than the freelancer preferred it to reveal up, and grocery buying have emerge as a want. It made it smooth to mention who cares approximately paintings until the traumatic time of payday arrived and there has been a whole lot much less work and therefore a wonderful deal less coins.

You do need humans for your existence who are going to push you to be greater a fulfillment or to have amusing, however it desires to be balanced. The individual who is constantly negative, who talks all of the manner all of the manner right down to you or continually has a backhand statement is the person you want to lessen out of your existence or limit your contact with.

To stay stimulated, you need parents which might be going to face in the decrease lower back of you. They are going to be proud whilst you make the small goals. Sometimes they're going to make errors in not emphasizing how they enjoy, however commonplace, they may generally be there for you.

The secret is to permit the relationships you have help you even as you need the aid. Friendship have to be a two-manner street, however too frequently friends make excuses for why they do no longer call. One won't understand while the pleasant time is. Another might be suffering from a health trouble. A zero.33 friend also can have kids, despite the fact that the buddy does not work, all the pal can appear to do is awareness at the kids in preference to buddies. Notice that the ones statements could be biased.

Until you ask, you in no way understand what is going on along with your friends and relying on your stress they'll be reluctant to percent theirs as it'd seem paltry to your situations.

You may be the one that continuously contacts your buddies. At least, when you use your motivation to accomplish that, you recognize you've got were given time to speak. You can guide your friends and allow them to useful resource you.

There are best and horrific relationships. Sometimes the decreasing remarks made through a partner, buddy, or little one makes you more encouraged to reveal them wrong. The truth of this element is that you take the assertion for what it's far. You determine the situation, decide in case you are taking too prolonged to meet the aim, and start running on it once more to reveal the individual wrong. You can not stay on the assertion made.

It is notable while you gain great feedback. When a exquisite remark is made, you get to live on it as an entire lot as you need even as you preserve taking place the duties you want to complete.

Last Thoughts on Motivation

1.Kick the negatives to the reduce.

2.Dwell, wallow, and bounce with happiness at any of the positives.

three.Accept mistakes stand up and circulate on.

four.Meet small goals, so you experience glad that you could do subjects, and paintings toward the larger desires.

five.To ensure motivation, make a bigger intention a chain of small accomplishments, and reward your self both with material matters or phrases.

# Chapter 10: Ingredients to Grow Your Confidence

We have reached the element of discussing some self notion building guidelines to help make sure that your non-public boom and self-motivation hold growing beneath a "inexperienced thumb."

1.Anxiety is a part of the cycle. This problem can't be pressured sufficient. You need a piece anxiety to perform better. In small doses tension is useful, however at the same time as you allow your worry get the better of you it will become counterproductive. Use your strain, sadness, or dissatisfied to be the push that makes you endorsed and assured.

2.Certainty in which you do no longer doubt your competencies or 2d wager yourself is vital. We all have instances whilst we doubt ourselves. You are going to investigate approaches to get spherical the ones feelings, however the factors for self belief are feeling fact.

three.Pride is each distinctive manner to experience confident. If you could take delight inside the work, relationships, or factors of your existence then you could agree with.

4.Safety is a need to have, wherein you want to feel you're constant in any scenario. When you sense stable or cushty, you can lighten up and specific your skills and feelings less complicated.

five.Confidence hinges on happiness. If you consider you studied high-quality of the negatives, then you definitely definately definately aren't satisfied. If you continuously allow fear and fears, along aspect terrible attitudes plague you, happiness and because of this self perception isn't going to boom.

6.Love yourself. If you do now not love who you're, then it's miles going to be difficult for all people else to look your actually worth.

Now that you recognize the additives to help yourself belief broaden allow's speak about how you could artwork to put into effect them for a more assured, and consequently a more introduced on you.

Tips for Self-Assurance

Feeling sure approximately your talents may be some thing that comes and is going. Let's pass another time to the example of the girl who by using threat mischarged a client. To lessen the tension about the scenario, she commenced out to remember her art work life, and the way regularly this type of mistake had happened. When she idea approximately it, it had in no way came about earlier than. It made it smooth to dismiss and discover reality that she is succesful, but she did not pay sufficient interest.

● Think approximately awards you've got gotten in college or work.

● Consider a praise someone gave you.

● Assess the truth of a state of affairs. Another example is of our freelancer. She doubted the potential to put in writing books and get them posted. Knowing a tale in her thoughts modified into on the lame facet, greater romance and mob associated thriller, she nevertheless determined to put up it online. Going through with that and thinking about that it receives look at each now and again, is enough to assist guarantee her that a person reachable desires to take a look at her matters. On the opportunity side of factors, you do want to keep in mind your skills and be unbiased. It is going again to the restrictions you might have. If you are wonderful approximately the volume of abilities, then being much less than a few different or your struggles are simply popular.

When you advantage reality and reduce your strain, you will sense more secure in situations that take a look at your skills and self guarantee. You may even discover ways to awareness at the happiness in preference to the negatives. Just as you take into account your accomplishments, possibly your first rate grades or awards for nice subjects, you may discover the love you've got were given for yourself.

Until you want yourself, you are not going if you need to get maintain of it from every one-of-a-kind character or maybe deliver it. Confidence comes from internal and in case you are hinging your "specialness" on extraordinary humans to your lifestyles, it is time to trade. Use the talents referred to above to create a way that works with the intention to love your self.

For the belongings you are not in reality glad with, art work on small desires, praise the modifications, push your motivation inside the path of gaining more self guarantee, and recall it does take artwork. You will not alternate in a single day.

Some morning you'll wake up feeling higher approximately yourself. You are going to have greater power to finish obligations, no matter the truth that they're mundane.

Final Tips

1.Make positive there aren't any fitness-related motives you experience depressed or disappointed in yourself.

2.Work on small goals first.

3.Reward the small accomplishments.

4.Award yourself with a higher reward at the same time as the purpose is big.

five.Motivation, anxiety, and self notion are the cycle, wherein tension pushes you to emerge as extra encouraged and therefore your self belief grows with finished duties.

6.You are who you're, fine you may alternate, and your mind is the powerful tool that makes it take area.

Whether you operate a reflect, mag, or internal thoughts hold telling yourself that you are worthwhile, you exist because you recall if handiest to your self, and you've got were given have been given the electricity to obtain any aim you choice.

## Chapter 11: Why Do Some People Have Motivation?

Motivation and why a few humans have seem to have greater than others.

Quite definitely, the dictionary defines motivation as a cause or reasons for appearing or behaving in a particular way.

Sound quite easy while we positioned it like that!

In reality motivation is a few thing however easy, for maximum people it's a every day conflict between what they want to do and what they do or don't revel in like doing.The line among motivation and self place is a blurry one. Generally speaking if we've got got have been given a right passion for the mission to be had motivation comes quite effortlessly, in particular if it's in reference to a few aspect you in reality love.

It is probably that traditional vehicle you've been restoring, the e-book you've been writing or a very selfless act which embody coaching your infant to revel in a motorbike. That tough work of love will get you coming again time after time and to a massive amount irrespective of the consequences that you get along the way. The special extremes are the ones moments while you may simply need to be doing some thing other than the mission handy, as an example that moment at the same time as you pull lower back the bed sheets on a cold January morning understanding that a five mile run awaits you or that company report you've been putting off in the long run have to be completed nowadays.

The element that gadgets absolutely recommended human beings apart from the less endorsed among is they WILL do the second batch of duties; the run can be the super ever, that document could have colleagues amazed at the level of element or destiny plans held inner it. Simply rolling over in bed or calling into work unwell are not an choice. Successful people have the self disciple to do what desires to be achieved whilst it wishes to be completed and comply with their extensively encouraged country of thoughts to make sure it's completed well.

To the outdoor global those human beings who've the excellent jobs, biggest homes and flashiest cars appear like they have got all of it and that the entirety absolutely comes clean...nicely, it doesn't. Quite honestly they may be stimulated via using their dreams and the massive picture to the thing that they've so accurate at getting executed what needs to get accomplished they make it look smooth.

They have the equal struggles as each person else however they have the inducement and self subject to thrive a few factor life throws at them, failure is a getting to know possibility, a fixed decrease back is treasured remarks and every sadness is a using force for the subsequent attempt.

For 15 years, former Starbucks President Michelle Gaas has set her alarm for four:30 a.M. To head taking walks and regularly works until 10 or eleven at night, at the out of doors she seems like she a wealthy successful man or woman and those might aspire to be in her role. They don't however need to get up 3 hours earlier than her or stay at artwork 5 hours later to get there.

Do you think on those bloodless January mornings there isn't the strange day that she may be capable of't be afflicted to move on foot or she gets to 4pm a few paintings days understanding she nonetheless has five meetings to go until home time and seems like she may additionally need to simply faux to be a bit beneath the weather then bypass home early. Of path there may be, she's human! But as with simply a achievement and inspired humans at with a view to I/wont I second she thinks of her goals and the big photo of what she is making an attempt to gain and gets through it.

As we touched on a 2d ago motivation varies and you can definitely experience extra caused for duties that truely need to do, that why it's vitally critical that to the exceptional of your functionality you fill your days with a project, profession or purpose that gets your juices flowing and makes you need to do extra and get higher. Life doesn't want to be a war to attain first rate matters if over the years you observe the ones internal appropriate and horrible feeling that your thoughts offers you withon a each day foundation and you comply with them to a few element you're surely obsessed on. It perhaps which you'rein a challenge which you don't like at present or a stay ahouse you enjoy isn't up to conventional. The very method of focusing on growing your motivation and striving to for change will enhance your thoughts-set no cease, lengthy earlier than you honestly get that dream hobby or nicer residence. Progression in the direction of your dreams is the vital element reward, as you development you'll see your self growing into the person you've continuously dreamt of and slowly but virtually you could start to understand you're one of the people you used to have a take a look at and suppose wow, I want I became like them!

So, now we comprehend motivation isn't a few factor that truly falls into your lap or some magical tremendous that successful humans have in abundance we may want to get right down to the realistic additives you downloaded this e-book for.

How are you capable of boom your motivation?

## Chapter 12: How to Set Goals

"You need a plan to gather a house. To construct a existence, it is even extra critical to have a plan or goal." – Zig Ziglar

Goals make sure you get the extraordinary out of life, for 2 motives.

Firstly, thru way of turning into a higher person, your new determined information and skills assist you to enjoy more out of the same existence activities compared to the previous you. Think approximately how your worldview is precise now vs the you 10 years within the beyond. Do you notice existence with an lousy lot more clarity, intensity and angle these days than you have got been within the past? What can be a easy each day prevalence within the past holds masses extra meaning to the extra appreciably advanced you these days.

Secondly, time passes in our lifestyles, whether or not or now not we need to or not. Goals with unique measures and cut-off dates ensure we're maximizing our output and reports in the course of our time right here. If you've got have been given already determined your existence purpose, your desires will make certain you get the nice out of your reason.

Goal placing is the first step in the course of a hit purpose success. It marks your first element inside the course of success. It is what located your life into real movement mode. Without this step, the possibility steps of purpose fulfillment cannot take region.

Have you ever encountered human beings who have a passive approach closer to life? They don't set any goals and they simply stay existence on a meandering, regular foundation. You see them 1 one year, three years, 5 years from now, and their lives are in large detail the identical, keep for some adjustments which can be sincerely extra the prevent result of others' actions and desires in location in their very own.

Setting your goals offers you clarity on what you in the end want and it ensures which you are channeling some time, strength and efforts into subjects that virtually rely variety to you. It makes you live greater consciously. Everything on this global is created times: First – introduction on your mind, discovered with the aid of manner of the manifestation in truth. Without the highbrow creation, there might be no bodily advent. When you put a motive, you've already finished half of the art work!

The thing at the same time as you put desires marks one the points while you are maximum related collectively together with your supply of motivation. It is even as your motivation is at its pinnacle. Having dreams at your aspect feature regular reminders of your motivational assets. They are the gas which pressure you beforehand and preserve you going whilst the going receives difficult.

So, we understand how vital desires are sincerely how can we set them?

The very motion of you searching for this ebook manner which you are the form of character who's thinking about your achievement and achievements in life. With that during mind I will hold this section pretty concise for a couple of reasons, first of all as you're the form of man or woman who's looking for books like this you have got got have been given likely already set a few desires and now you want assist to acquire them, secondly as reason setting is a massive trouble you may without troubles dedicate a whole e-book to it in it's non-public right.

For those who have not had been given set goals worry not, a clean search on line receives you numerous reason putting sources at the clicking of a button.

One of the maximum widely known aim placing techniques is the usage of the SMART additives, you may have already used or heard of this but in essence it is a manner of making sure your goals are the following:

Specific

Measurable

Attainable

Realistic

Timely

Specific: A specific goal has a much more risk of being completed than a modern-day aim. To set a particular aim you need to reply the six "W" questions:

*Who:     Who is concerned?

*What:    What do I need to perform?

*Where:   Identify an area.

*When:    Establish a time body.

*Which:   Identify requirements and constraints.

*Why:     Specific reasons, reason or advantages of conducting the intention.

EXAMPLE: A desired reason might be, "Get in shape." But a specific cause may say, "Join a gymnasium and exercising three days steady with week."

Measurable - Establish concrete necessities for measuring development towards the attainment of every aim you place.

When you measure your improvement, you stay on the right track, attain your intention dates, and experience the pride of achievement that spurs you on to persevered attempt required to gain your aim.

To decide if your purpose is measurable, ask questions consisting of……

How masses? How many?

How will I apprehend while it is finished?

Attainable – When you pick out dreams which is probably most important to you, you begin to figure out techniques you may lead them to return actual. You increase the attitudes, talents, abilties, and financial capability to achieve them. You start seeing formerly ignored opportunities to carry yourself closer to the achievement of your dreams.

You can attain most any cause you located at the same time as you suggest your steps appropriately and set up a time frame that allows you to carry out those steps. Goals that might have appeared far away and out of reach ultimately pass nearer and turn out to be workable, now not because of the fact your desires reduce back, however due to the reality you grow and expand to fit them. When you list your dreams you build your self-photo. You see yourself as clearly worth of these desires, and growth the traits and persona that let you private them.

Realistic- To be realistic, a goal should represent an aim in the direction of that you are each inclined and in a function to paintings. A goal can be every excessive and sensible; you're the simplest person who can determine simply how excessive your intention need to be. But make sure that every aim represents super development.

A immoderate goal is frequently less hard to collect than a low one due to the fact a low goal exerts low motivational pressure. Some of the hardest jobs you ever performed simply appear clean surely due to the fact they have been a hard paintings of love.

Timely – A reason need to be grounded inside a time frame. With no time frame tied to it there's no experience of urgency. If you want to lose 10 lbs, at the same time as do you need to lose it by way of the usage of? "Someday" obtained't paintings. But in case you anchor it interior a time frame, "thru May 1st", then you definitely've set your subconscious mind into motion to start working on the intention.

Your reason is probably realistic in case you truly trust that it may be executed. Additional techniques to comprehend in case your cause is sensible is to decide if you have executed a few factor similar inside the past or ask yourself what conditions might should exist to carry out this purpose.

Use the SMART technique to begin to don't forget your desires over the subsequent week, month, yr, 5 years and so on. Visualize on your very very own mind precisely what you want to reap and what you want life to be like for you and your own family. Spend a while by myself thinking about this and make sure to put in writing down your thoughts. It doesn't need to be a hundred% accurate as dreams can constantly be changed and amended but the critical detail is to get in down on paper or stored for your phone or PC so you can speak with it as and at the same time as required.

Taking that a step similarly at some point of the following bankruptcy we're able to consider a way to technique each day to maximise your intention associated sports that will help you advantage tremendous achievement.

Keeping a mag is an remarkable manner of improving your lifestyles in fashionable and also assisting you to live targeted for your dreams whilst studying out of your set backs. Every day I start the day with the aid of the usage of writing out a listing of the responsibilities and achievements I want to fulfil that day and drift them off as I circulate. I have no concept why but the actual mechanical motion of crossing off devices is fun – perhaps because in a few deep down subconscious location of our brains it's a manner of retaining rating and just like playing on a video video games console or cellular phone app anybody want to get the immediate gratification that achieving a task offers us.

Slowly however absolutely the longer I used the method every day my to do listing might also get a piece longer and each night time time I have to look back at the topics I controlled to get finished and complete my magazine with thoughts for the day. Without certainly thinking about it I commenced out out a way of completing my maximum urgent sports on a every day basis. The award winning author Brian Tracy says "DO THE WORST, FIRST" and that's precisely what I did.

Each day I might do the jobs I hated the most to begin with and then slowly get to the plenty much less exhausting duties. Be high-quality to include obligations collectively with workout and excellent time with own family as despite the truth that they may be cast off that day retaining a wholesome body and top own family relationships should be commonplace long term dreams for anyone.

A mag and to-do listing have become one of the satisfactory movements I ever made and a fantastic addiction I nonetheless maintain to this very day.

## Chapter 13: Daily Motivation and Goal Setting

Each day has 24 hours.

Err, positive. Obviously you're possibly wondering to your self however the key factor of that statement is that all of us have the equal quantity of time in a day; Donald Trump has 24 hours much like the man who's been on foot at the same gas station on your neighborhood for the final 10 years has 24 hours. That's no longer to say that strolling in gasoline station is terrible, in reality not if that became his purpose however the element is that there may be no magic time creation gadget. We all have a restrained quantity of time useful useful resource and we should do our outstanding to use it accurately.

This brings us onto one of the number one hurdles one have to overcome to achieve success…..Mornings.

If you google any particularly successful person there may be a totally immoderate hazard that you could discover they have got advanced the dependancy of waking up early and attacking the day with gusto, be it getting their education consultation finished in advance than most humans even awaken or truely getting started out on their workload for that day.

While I'm not announcing you need to be getting up at four:30am every day to move on foot with Michelle Gaas the mornings may be one in each of your most green components of your day and right here's why.

You are lots much less possibly to get distracted inside the morning. A a fulfillment, particularly recommended man or woman's day fills up fast. If you wait until the afternoon or night time to do some issue sizable for yourself on the side of exercise or reading, you're probably to push it off the to-do listing altogether. Distractions have hundreds a good deal an awful lot much less hazard of developing at 6 a.M. So get began early!

You have more willpower early in the day. Even in case you are not a morning character,

129

you can have more strength of will inside the early hours than later inside the day. During the direction of the day as you are dealing with hard human beings, making decisions and preventing site visitors, you dissipate your self-control, leaving you feeling depleted inside the path of the forestall of the day.

Mornings come up with the opportunity to set a pleasing tone for the day. If you've got ever slept in past your alarm clock that taking off the day with a failure can deliver down your temper and feature an effect to your productivity at paintings. Waking up in advance and right away beginning to gain your desires lets in you to start the day with a victory and set the tone for a happier and in addition powerful day.

With that in mind now what, your up early and want to acquire however a manner to you flow into about developing that all important to do listing?

And in what order do you simply do stuff?

Brain Tracy have turn out to be one of the first self assist authors I located and to quote the man or woman himself -"Write it down. Your goals need to be in writing. They have to be clean, specific, unique and measurable. You need to write out your desires as if you had been setting an order on your purpose to be artificial in a manufacturing unit at a brilliant distance. Make your description easy and specific in every experience"

Personally I simply write out my dreams on a bit of A4 paper and bypass them off as I skip, the order in which you move them off can variety from in reality"doing the worst first"or the usage of more scientific strategies certainly one of which I'll cover underneath.

The ABC method as practiced via the usage of Brian Tracy

The greater idea you invest in planning and putting priorities earlier than you begin, the greater critical matters you could do and the faster you can get them finished whilst you get commenced.

The extra critical and treasured the assignment is to you, the extra you will be endorsed to triumph over procrastination and release your self into the system.

The ABC Method is a powerful priority setting technique that you can use each unmarried day. This approach is so easy and powerful that it may, all via the usage of itself, make you one of the maximum inexperienced and powerful human beings to your place.

The electricity of this method lies in its simplicity. Here's how it works: You start with a listing of the whole thing you need to do for the imminent day. Think on paper. You then vicinity an A, B, or C in advance than every item for your listing earlier than you begin the primary venture.

An "A" item is described as a few issue that is very critical. This is some issue which you have to do. This is a undertaking for which there may be intense results in case you do it or fail to do it, like journeying a key customer or completing a file for your boss that she dreams for an upcoming board assembly.

If you have got a couple of"A"assignment, you prioritize those responsibilities thru writing A-1, A-2, A-three, and so on in front of every object.

A"B"object is described as a challenge which you ought to do. But it terrific has mild effects. This manner that someone may be unhappy or inconvenienced in case you don't do it, however it is nowhere as crucial as an"A"assignment. Returning an unimportant phone message or reviewing your email may be a"B"assignment. The rule is that you need to in no manner do a"B"project even as there's an"A"project left undone.

 A"C"project is defined as a few issue that is probably superb to do, but for which there aren't any effects in any respect, whether or no longer you do it or now not."C"responsibilities include phoning a friend, having coffee or lunch with a coworker or completing a few personal agency throughout paintings hours. This shape of hobby has no have an impact on in any respect to your paintings life.

After you have done the ABC Method on your listing, you can now be honestly prepared and organized to get extra important things finished faster.

The mystery to meaking this ABC Method work is so one can now discipline your self to begin at once on your"A-1"task and then stay at it until it is whole. Use your strength of thoughts to get going and live going on this one venture, the maximum essential unmarried challenge you can probably be doing. Eat the entire frog anddon't save you till it's finished absolutely.

Your ability to think through, analyzeyour artwork list and decide your"A-1"venture is the springboard to better degrees of achievement, and extra conceitedness, self-recognize and private pleasure.

Review you figure listing right now and placed an A, B, or C subsequent to each challenge or hobby. Select your A-1 challenge or undertaking and begin on it without delay. Discipline yourself to do now not anything else until this one interest is entire.

Practice this ABC Method every day and on each artwork or undertaking listing, in advance than you start paintings, for the following month. By that time, you can have superior the addiction of placing and jogging on your maximum precedence obligations and your future can be assured!

## Chapter 14: Maintaining motivation for the long time

Naturally our motivation ranges vary over time, occasionally it can be now not some thing to do with the technique your really doing, as an instance in case you've had an difficulty with a member of the family 20 minutes earlier than your favourite TV display comes on in spite of the truth which you continue to love the show your unlikely to experience it as a whole lot as you usually do.

To a degree the ones difficult days are whilst you absolutely ought to dig deep and certainly get thru relying almost mostly on self concern. Thankfully those surely lousy days are uncommon and for nearly all of the time any issues you have were given in terms of keeping motivation will really be the age antique hassle that everyone have of in truth preserving that passion and zest for lifestyles.

It is crucial to create an environment that fosters motivation, and allows it to thrive. When going through all of the hassle to prep yourself for the following degree for your existence, there may be no component in having your environment push you off beam. This may also furthermore require you to make a few drastic modifications. However, in the end, it's going to possibly be properly well really worth your on the identical time as.

You'll want to begin with the useful resource of tackling the place you spend the most time in. If your intention is to shed pounds, or get in higher shape, then your first step have to be ridding your private home of all useless temptations.

☐     Do you have were given a candy drawer? Empty it out!

☐     Are the tubs on top of tubs of ice cream within the freezer? Get rid of them?

So, what takes area for your next experience to the grocery hold? Go immediately to healthy, do no longer pass junk meals aisle, do now not collect chips and cookies. Yes, the ones vibrant shades and the reminiscence of the 'crunch of satisfaction' will have you ever ever ever trying to scoop the contents off all of the shelves into your cart. Be strong even though!

Jot down the substances of your desired healthful recipes and make that the focus of your buying revel in. Don't simply browse thru the aisles, strut thru them with a purpose.

Although the instance above applies to food it can be amended to simply any terrible distraction, for instance maximum human beings inside the superior global now have get admission to to the net and plenty of use it for paintings. How easy is it to open a contemporary tab and take a look at Twitter or Facebook? Yep. Very easy! Before you do keep in mind your to do listing and what you need to collect that day to acquire your desires, with the aid of all manner if your list is achieved watch T.V, circulate on Facebook however get the large stuff finished first and then reward yourself.

If your aim is to turn out to be a more effective person, then the skills you're looking for is probably organizational competencies. Once all once more, your own home should be your place to start.

☐      What does your table appear like?

☐      Is your handbag or pockets complete of three hundred and sixty five days vintage receipts?

☐      Do you've got were given piles of paper placing round aimlessly within the filing cupboard?

Get the shredder out, inventory up on folders and labels and located your self to artwork.

You will, but, need to be practical approximately how a bargain you can get completed in a day/week. Whereas emptying out a sweet drawer may additionally take a few seconds, filing administrative center paintings can be loads more tedious and soak up a vast quantity of time. In such situations, it is important to be sensible and avoid being overwhelmed. Easier stated than finished? Not, always.

One of the primary motives why getting prepared looks as if a project for plenty, is because of the truth that they're looking to condense a years definitely properly really worth of disorganization into one week and normally, one day. This will most effective hose down your spirits and reason you to drag out a hair or  in the manner. Rather than dumping all the contents of each and each drawer at the ground, and saying to your self, 'I'm not preventing till the final paper is tucked thoroughly into the folder,' begin small.

• Get a timer

• Set the timer to among 15 and 30 minutes

• Get out as a good deal as you keep in mind you studied will preserve you occupied all through that point

• Set the tone collectively together with your favorite tracks booming in the history

• Let the filing begin

• Ding! Once the timer stops, you're completed. Any piece of paper no longer filed, shall be tucked lower lower back into the drawer for any other day.

Continue this habitual for the following few days, and right away, your workspace can be certainly as prepared because it desires to be.

If you are attempting to make huge strides every now and then you can't do it by myself, you need manual. Earlier we touched on the instance of Donald Trump and the man at the gas station, one of the key versions modified into Donald Trump were given some assist, he took people on and outsourced what he may additionally moreover need to to others. The actual nature of your goals will determine who you need round you, it may be a non-public teacher or existence teach, it may even clearly be a friend or employer of friends with not unusual hobbies or similar dreams.

Get the assist you need. No you possibly can deny that taking on a trendy lifestyle or difficult yourself is much less complicated at the same time as you have someone with the useful resource of your thing with the same dreams set inside the the the front of them. Speak together along with your family and pals about this new stage of motivation and achievement that you're eager on assignment and encourage someone who you take delivery of as real with could be concerned to join in. Your own family and pals will definitely offer you all the resource within the international and having humans spherical you who're aware about your desires may be honestly the spark you need to keep going despite the fact that things get hard.

With a person thru way of your component, you will have simply the frenzy you want while you are not feeling very assured or inspired and you may additionally be capable of return the determine upon for this person while they're having a down day. Being held liable for your dreams and providing management to others when they want to be held responsible is considered in reality one of lifestyles's real motivating factors. No-one wants to seem like a failure inside the eyes in their pals or circle of relatives so setting it available may be a terrific device, positive they're may be some naysayers who doubt you or are secretly (or no longer so secretly) hoping you fail however who cares, use it as gas to strain your self to achieve. If someone doubts your capabilities to achieve your desires and keep your degrees of motivation greater often than not it's a mirrored photo on their internal feelings about their stages of success or self doubt in desire to something to do with you. The outstanding component you may do in that situation is actually gain what you set out to do and display to them that it may be accomplished. You also can actually grow to be a characteristic model to them inside the future.

An vital part of keeping the motivation is not giving yourself reasons why you have to huff, puff, and blow it out your very very very own motivational hearth. You want to maintain the manner as a laugh and as appealing as feasible. The least quantity of pressure that you come upon alongside the manner, the higher your opportunities are at sticking to the plan and task your long term desires.

Positivity

Above all, stay high nice. All horrible power should be left somewhere very far out of your breathing area. You'll want to surround yourself with wonderful humans, effective reminiscences and exceptional thoughts.

## Chapter 15: What if…..

So, you've observe as much as right right right here.

What if you're in spite of the truth that not precipitated?

What if I you fail?

What if subjects don't cross to plan?

The best failure you want to ever take transport of is the act of failure itself. The beyond is in the lower back of you. All the ones errors that have been made, all of the struggles you went via, use them as in addition motivational gear to do better next time.

These bumps in the road need to in no manner be allowed to puncture your tires over again due to the truth now, at this gift second, you realise wherein they're and also you recognize certainly the direction to take to keep away from them. Face these days and the following day with a grin.

Bring passion back for your lifestyles and enjoy a rejuvenation to be able to gasoline you with all of the motivation you need to keep that smile on via every hurdle you bypass and every intention you accomplish. You are the best one on top of factors of your destiny and with the proper thoughts-set, concrete desires, enough ardour and self motivation, you may be the person you've got constantly preferred to be and allow your relationships with all components of your lifestyles to flourish into some problem lovely due to it.

The relationship you've got were given with your self is likewise an vital one. Being content material with the man or woman you're and having the ardour to meet all your dreams and make your goals a reality is some issue you ought to constantly reason to have at its height. Life is simply too brief and the arena is in reality too lovely to sit down down down lower back and permit time to pass with the resource of. Be adventurous, gain deep down and find out the incentive you need to triumph over every day like a champion. Whether it is a new challenge which you need to test your competencies in, a cutting-edge career route which you'd like to deal with, or virtually an area of your existence which you'd need to ignite, don't appearance beforehand to the next day, located the changes into motion in recent times.

If your nonetheless struggling with motivation, goal placing and clearly typically getting began remember getting out a sheet of paper, go somewhere quiet in which you wont be interrupted and consider the following.

Have you identified the hassle?

☐    I think so

☐    I'm not pretty certain what the problem is

☐    I do not realize wherein to start

☐    Absolutely

Have you normal that a change wants to be made?

☐     I can't trade

☐     I want to make a trade I virtually do not apprehend how

☐     I'm thinking about developing a exchange

☐     I've located my mind to it and absolutely set up that a alternate wants to be made

What modifications do you want to make in your existence?

What is your largest fear?

How do you triumph over this worry?

What are your short-time period goals?

•     How will you accomplish them?

What are your long time desires?

•     How will you accomplish them?

Keep this bit of paper in a secure location because the answers to the ones questions are vitally crucial to you - hold them as a reminder of what you're going for walks inside the course of.

You also can encourage yourself thru inspirational fees and success memories. Numerous pretty a achievement human beings have had large u.S.A.And downs. Buy a few autobiographies or maybe take a look at a few Wikipedia articles on those who you've got regarded as tons as in the past otherwise you revel in are excessive achievers. You might be surprised at how many have had struggles way beyond what you are managing and feature in reality kept setting one foot in the front of the alternative and marched towards their desires.

Each week, choose a person and permit their story to encourage you and bring you toward your purpose. They possibly did a similar hassle when they had been seeking out motivation and appearance how their tale grew to become out!No-one wants to seem like a failure inside the eyes in their pals or circle of relatives so setting it available may be a terrific device, positive they're may be some naysayers who doubt you or are secretly (or no longer so secretly) hoping you fail however who cares, use it as gas to strain your self to achieve. If someone doubts your capabilities to achieve your desires and keep your degrees of motivation greater often than not it's a mirrored photo on their internal feelings about their stages of success or self doubt in desire to something to do with you. The outstanding component you may do in that situation is actually gain what you set out to do and display to them that it may be accomplished. You also can actually grow to be a characteristic model to them inside the future.

An vital part of keeping the motivation is not giving yourself reasons why you have to huff, puff, and blow it out your very very very own motivational hearth. You want to maintain the manner as a laugh and as appealing as feasible. The least quantity of pressure that you come upon alongside the manner, the higher your opportunities are at sticking to the plan and task your long term desires.

Positivity

Above all, stay high nice. All horrible power should be left somewhere very far out of your breathing area. You'll want to surround yourself with wonderful humans, effective reminiscences and exceptional thoughts.

## Chapter 16: What if…..

So, you've observe as much as right right right here.

What if you're in spite of the truth that not precipitated?

What if I you fail?

What if subjects don't cross to plan?

The best failure you want to ever take transport of is the act of failure itself. The beyond is in the lower back of you. All the ones errors that have been made, all of the struggles you went via, use them as in addition motivational gear to do better next time.

These bumps in the road need to in no manner be allowed to puncture your tires over again due to the truth now, at this gift second, you realise wherein they're and also you recognize certainly the direction to take to keep away from them. Face these days and the following day with a grin.

Bring passion back for your lifestyles and enjoy a rejuvenation to be able to gasoline you with all of the motivation you need to keep that smile on via every hurdle you bypass and every intention you accomplish. You are the best one on top of factors of your destiny and with the proper thoughts-set, concrete desires, enough ardour and self motivation, you may be the person you've got constantly preferred to be and allow your relationships with all components of your lifestyles to flourish into some problem lovely due to it.

The relationship you've got were given with your self is likewise an vital one. Being content material with the man or woman you're and having the ardour to meet all your dreams and make your goals a reality is some issue you ought to constantly reason to have at its height. Life is simply too brief and the arena is in reality too lovely to sit down down down lower back and permit time to pass with the resource of. Be adventurous, gain deep down and find out the incentive you need to triumph over every day like a champion. Whether it is a new challenge which you need to test your competencies in, a cutting-edge career route which you'd like to deal with, or virtually an area of your existence which you'd need to ignite, don't appearance beforehand to the next day, located the changes into motion in recent times.

If your nonetheless struggling with motivation, goal placing and clearly typically getting began remember getting out a sheet of paper, go somewhere quiet in which you wont be interrupted and consider the following.

Have you identified the hassle?

☐ I think so

☐ I'm not pretty certain what the problem is

☐ I do not realize wherein to start

☐ Absolutely

Have you normal that a change wants to be made?

☐        I can'trade

☐        I want to make a trade I virtually do not apprehend how

☐        I'm thinking about developing a exchange

☐        I've located my mind to it and absolutely set up that a alternate wants to be made

What modifications do you want to make in your existence?

What is your largest fear?

How do you triumph over this worry?

What are your short-time period goals?

•        How will you accomplish them?

What are your long time desires?

•        How will you accomplish them?

Keep this bit of paper in a secure location because the answers to the ones questions are vitally crucial to you - hold them as a reminder of what you're going for walks inside the course of.

You also can encourage yourself thru inspirational fees and success memories. Numerous pretty a achievement human beings have had large u.S.A.And downs. Buy a few autobiographies or maybe take a look at a few Wikipedia articles on those who you've got regarded as tons as in the past otherwise you revel in are excessive achievers. You might be surprised at how many have had struggles way beyond what you are managing and feature in reality kept setting one foot in the front of the alternative and marched towards their desires.

Each week, choose a person and permit their story to encourage you and bring you toward your purpose. They possibly did a similar hassle when they had been seeking out

motivation and appearance how their tale
grew to become out!

## Chapter 17: What is Motivation?

Welcome to the first monetary break of this e-book. This part of the ebook might be handling a tough information of the idea of motivation and its importance in existence. Pretty fundamental sounding, this bankruptcy has been specifically written to make you hold close the idea of motivation. You have been warned; do not anticipate whatever first rate to investigate from this chapter. However, in case you need to peep into what motivation is and what importance it holds to your life, take a look at on and discover!

Motivation is a pressure that courses one to do what one does. Motivation is the motive at the back of human movements. What you do, assume, say and act is all inspired and originating from someplace. Have you ever pondered approximately the supply of all your actions? It isn't clearly the moves, however furthermore the repetitions of 1's movements which might be pushed through motivation. When you are recommended enough, you're organized to head all of the manner and grab the factor you've got typically desired or wished for.

As it is simple apparent, the word Motivation has been derived from the word 'reason'. 'Motive' may be superb defined because the real purpose inside the again of someone's movement. It want to no longer b forced with its cousin 'Intention' that may be a completely precise concept altogether. Let me offer you with an instance to distinguish amongst reason and purpose.

Frank is an unemployed guy in his twenties who has two youngsters to feed and a family to govern. Helpless, he turns to mugging and sooner or later comes throughout a rich businessman who has were given large quantity of dollars stashed in his bulging wallet. Frank takes out his mugging knife and darts inside the route of the character.

In the above scenario, the motive of our problem, Frank is to thing the knife and loot the businessman. However, Frank's cause is to feed his starving youngsters. Motive is a larger set than intention. It is the actual cause at the back of any precise motion. Hence, motivation may be more or less defined because of the truth the actual purpose or push that makes a person perform what he plays, and thinks what he thinks. Hence, we end that motivation is a tremendous model of purpose this is going past on the spot want or preference.

The basis of Motivation has theories in particular Natural vs. Rational principle and principle. Let us have a short expertise of what every of them has to mention on the problem.

Nature has bestowed man with awesome survival instincts. Because of the equal, some element moves guy does in the long run is, consciously or otherwise, aimed toward surviving or "making the evolutionary reduce". On the alternative hand, guy, through statement revel in and capabilities, achieves powers of rational thinking and making correct alternatives. These powers of mind are not dispensed amongst all in addition. Not each person has the equal footing close to proudly owning rational-centric powers.

Advocates of each principle argue that it's far their declare that wins over the alternative. Nature whilst blessing mankind with survival instincts extended its software to getting stimulated. One's motivations are derived from one's herbal instincts of survival. On the opportunity hand, the rational theory claims that every guy has had been given his personal set of skills relying on how a good buy he has labored closer to it. Motivation within the type of situation is derived from one's reviews and skills.

The 2nd precept is Content vs. Process principle, which goes like: Anything that you see is the cease result of an enter that has been converted into the preferred output through a tough and fast gadget of types. There is a specific gadget involved inside the entering life of some thing this is an final

161

outcomes of any type. Motivation whilst seen thru the prism of technique concept virtually calls for that there need to be high pleasant situations so as for it to be artificial.

On the possibility hand, the content fabric cloth concept argues that the situations for the a hit production of human motivation is based upon upon and range from situation to scenario. It is not crucial that the type and amount of motivation Howard receives or generates is the equal type and quantity generated or acquired through Amy. They variety no longer because of their destination but because of their deliver and the conditions that dictated their shipping.

Therefore, we've got come to recognize motivation not as a the usage of force, however as a squalling child whose beginning is determined with the resource of the situations surrounding the assignment. It is truely a the usage of strain, but first-class simply so. When you dig deeper, you can find out that it's miles a bargain extra than a stress; it is a associate.

## Chapter 18: Self-Motivation Kit

Welcome to the second one financial disaster of this ebook. This part of the ebook has been specially written if you want to equip you readers with the concept and practical additives of self-motivation. Without wasting an awful lot vicinity and time on gibberish, permit us to transport in addition.

We all require that extra push to move an inch in the route of victory, don't we? We aren't self-knowledgeable warriors who can address the whole thing life throws in our course. We are slaves to technology and have lost the historic and plenty wanted competencies to combat and stay to tell the tale. Asked to choose, we'd take a flight in location of stay lower decrease returned and combat for survival. Humans have began turning into less so. In this type of state of affairs, the need for self-motivation turns into pressing and vital.

The following a few lines will cope with the numerous approaches in which you can self-inspire your self. Usually it so takes region that almost about subjects related to personality or self-help, books motel to a series of generalized and too apparent guidelines. However, this a part of the e-book has been written preserving in mind the uselessness of such well-known advises.

Hold immediately to a Positive Thought

We are all little rays of mild. Despite how off track our lives emerge as, there are continuously moments in an afternoon even as we control to muster sufficient braveness to reflect onconsideration on something notable. Now, the primary diploma, i.E. Gathering excessive great thoughts is easy. However, the hard element is to hold on to them. It is important that something terrific you found, you maintain on with them. Do no longer permit glad thoughts wander with the aid of and get lost while you're busy in your each day life.

In order for this to seem, you have to allocate time. You can name this 'me-time'. Be it while cooking, taking a break from studies, sitting in the administrative center doing not anything or certainly analyzing the newspaper to your the the front garden; you can start collecting effective thoughts everywhere and on every occasion. However, allocation of a selected time ensures continuity and depth.

The Glass is Half Full

Remember the evergreen question about whether or not or no longer the glass is half complete or half of empty? It all is based upon at the manner you notice it. I ought to recommend you take a look at it as 1/2 of full. Being an positive is the excellent way to self-encourage oneself. When you have were given a study the brighter aspect of things, you mechanically push your self to desire. Hope is a strain that may win out of place wars and topple tyrannical empires. Make effective you adopt a non-bad thoughts-set toward lifestyles. Look for motives to be satisfied in the smallest of things. There may be a number of problems coming your manner. You cannot keep away from them. What you may do to restrict their impact on you is check their awesome elements. Remember to identify the silver lining on the cloud. A little little bit of optimism goes an prolonged way in finding out not simply your gift temper however moreover its impact for your normal productivity.

Set the Target

What is it which you are aiming for? Do you have were given an aim or a difficult and rapid of desires in mind? Are you simply blindly aiming for an unsure purpose within the darkish, groping for your bow and fumbling together along with your arrows?

In order to well and correctly encourage your self, you need to first sit down down down down and enlist all of your dreams. If you take a selected step, ensure you apprehend its destiny direction. Do not clearly do some element for the heck of it. Have a plan set in thoughts. The first step to all this is putting of desires. When you located your dreams, you come to be privy to your course. Everyone is supposed to be moving into a specific route. Have you located yours? When you 0 in to your path, you've got cause in lifestyles. This cause will lead you to your purpose. Your reason can be to carry out any right away hobby, which is meant to guide you in your purpose- undertaking a greater success. The difference amongst aim and cause is the distinction among intention and cause. Your intention is to come to be wealthy; your reason becomes doing agency or looking for a technique. Goals, therefore, are a large set on the same time as skills are their subsets.

Do no longer wander about aimlessly. You do greater damage with the useful resource of transferring earlier directionless than through the use of sitting idle doing not some thing. Take a while but make sure you come up with your own set of desires. Your goals want not be long term in nature. You need to set your goals even on an hourly basis. All you need to attend to is they need to not be unrealistic, openly ambitious or unachievable in the set time period and restricted useful aid to be had at your disposal.

Get Your Priorities Straight

Most motivational errors appear due to people no longer being capable of first, have priorities, and 2d, set them in order. A pizza shipping man's priority is attaining the holiday spot interior thirty mins. If he does not adhere to the norm, he has to give up the pizza for gratis, standing the danger to get fired through way of his boss. We all have comparable priorities to look after in life. If you fail to even apprehend them, you are certain to fail and motivation doesn't even start to take beginning.

Motivation comes from normal successes and successes require you to retaining your priority listing decluttered and managed. Unless you understand what you want to do and whilst, you're doomed. Motivation's largest supply being successes, it is going without saying that you need to now not exceptional discover your priorities but additionally paintings on organizing them in order of significance. Reading the newspaper may be less crucial than dropping your children to highschool. Dropping kids to school can be masses lots much less stressful a chore than getting geared up breakfast and so forth. Motivation is a ordinary phenomenon with every act which you do presenting you scopes, immediate and immediately ones, to advantage it.

A person with zero or disorganized priorities is destined for failure. When failures kicking on your each day existence everyday, you begin getting demotivated, depart by myself loss of motivation. The machine takes you in terrible in preference to there being a loss of motivation. This devices you again in slight years. Not most effective are you to work in the route of gaining motivation from zero onwards, you moreover may additionally must sweat your manner to first reach this hypothetical zero.

Aim For Small Objectives

Instead of going out all guns blazing from the word pass, you want to try to overcome the small but relevant victories. Winning is a exercise and exercising desires infant steps. These infant steps obtained't be possible when you have an intention to take advantage leaps. Tread slowly and attempt to obtain lots much less massive glories; people who require minimum attempt and but whilst accomplished supply most pride of having succeeded.

Here is how you could include the guideline of accomplishing small victories into your life:

☐ Prepare listing of everyday jobs like mowing the garden, giving the car for a wash, or attending a truly important place of business meeting. Having prepared this type of listing, you're now ready to prioritize.

☐ Decide which jobs are truly important, which ones are mildly so and which of them can be rescheduled or omitted to move returned to later. Your preference must rest upon how an entire lot significance every jobs holds for your existence.

☐   Now think of every such hobby as a touch victory. Every time you end a mission, strike them off your listing and flow into immediately to the subsequent one.

☐       Perform your day's paintings on this manner and you will in no way leave out out on finishing every venture that has been scheduled or assigned.

Motivation comes in small wallet. Therefore, on the same time as you accomplish the ones little wins as you walk on, you may understand that they add as a good deal as form a bulk strain that drives you in addition on the road to success.

Do Not Hesitate to Fail

Remember, the whole thing lousy that takes place to you takes vicinity for a motive. Life is entire of commands and there are awesome varieties of strategies as a way to examine them. One of the very effective ones is failing.

When you fail, it hits you difficult and you lay low for some time. You art work in your activity, teach your self more difficult and try to hit once more more potent. This is the way you gain motivation from screw ups. He who is failing does not even try the dive. He is afraid he received't make it to the alternative aspect; he refuses to take the soar.

Motivation is an end stop result. It is a completely closing product whose manufacturing ought to be preceded through some uncooked substances. Failure is one such vital raw cloth that is going into the production of self-motivation. Of course, no individual objectives to fail. So, how does one derive motivation from failure? We strive. Try with all you have got have been given were given and placed everything to your power into achieving what you're chasing. When you make investments your maximum into your efforts, you will locate which you  discover your self injected with a newfound braveness. This braveness isn't similar to the foolhardy form of courage. This braveness diminishes your barriers and units you unfastened. It permits you to take dangers and no longer appearance once more. Finally, you're capable of strive matters you'll no longer have attended before. All in all, in braveness you've got were given got positioned your actual motivation.

Look For Inspiration

Do no longer be ashamed to derive idea for the ones who've visible and done all of it. We people have continuously been installed upon others for topics. Food, secure haven or inspiration; we have got always derived them or inherited them from those who got here in advance than us. Read books approximately splendid folks who have been down in the ditch and decided to take subjects into their very private fingers and rose above the din to jot down down statistics. Famous authors who are capable of creating colourful photos in million of minds, great international leaders who led international locations to warfare and peace, awe inspiring conflict heroes who defended boundaries with all they had; such people in no way fail to inspire others in their personal quests.

Meditate

One very inexperienced technique of making sure which you prevent yourself from getting demotivated and hold gaining consistent excellent power is to meditate. Meditation permits you purchased a degree in which you not want to be privy to what's round you. You obtain a stage from wherein there can be no want on the way to look down and get yourself afflicted or worked up about what's taking region beneath; you're in a rustic of bliss and entire nothingness. Nothing that one says, does or thinks affects you in any manner anymore.

In this shape folks of a, you're enormously eligible to get hold of motivation power. Without you understanding, there exist outstanding energy round you in a shape hardly ever seen to the bare human eye. These energies need a medium or a manner to journey indoors your thoughts. They keep looking for a manner to come returned what might also moreover get indoors you however in no way discover any way in. When you meditate, you open yourself. Your obstacles are faded and your senses are heightened. Any small deviation in the normal state of affairs receives picked up through you. This is an first-rate degree for choosing up the ones remarkable vibes that have the capability to result in motivation indoors you.

Here is how you can use meditation to gain the loads-wanted motivation. Choose a old style area initially. Close all the house home windows and doorways; however, in case you are used to it with the aid of now, you may leave some window area open for air waft functions. Lay a mat on the ground and expect a skip-legged characteristic to take a seat down. After you have adjusted your feature, region each your arms on your knees, which is probably stretched to their most factors. Focus on a thing on the opposite wall. Keep focusing until your senses start leaving you. Do now not however fall proper into a rustic of fainting or sleep, as it'd defeat the very reason of meditating. Such practices gathers all exceptional energies mendacity spherical you and concentrates them to one location- your mind. Regular periods of the type of exercise should bring about not surely further strengthening of your thoughts energy however moreover reminiscence polishing.

Achieving of self-motivation isn't as herculean a assignment as being in the loop of having advocated. One can continuously discover ordinary examples of little motivation packets being executed in a few unspecified time in the future of the day. A easy piglet strolling across the farm may additionally want to encourage you. But the ones small inspirations are not anything on the undertaking of having a healthful impact on you and driving you within the course of grander victories in existence. The economic disaster has some truely green and foolproof techniques for achieving the appealing stimulated kingdom. I choice it proved informative similarly to a laugh as a manner to go through them fast. Wait no longer a 2nd and start inculcating them into your lifestyle.

## Chapter 19: Incorporation Of Motivation Into Your Personal Life

Welcome to the 1/three and final bankruptcy of this e-book. Once you have were given examine through the preceding chapters, you may recognise that motivation is not that massive a deal. It's no longer truely smooth to benefit however moreover an exquisite tool to have in this day of distress and allow downs. However, gaining motivation isn't always enough. You want to efficiently set up the incentive app on your existence if you want to ensure continuity. This bankruptcy is dedicated to train you all of the incredible techniques in which you may have a ordinary dose of motivation on foot into your device.

Emotion

Emotion, they're announcing is the strongest using stress. It might be anger, lust, love or sadness. Emotion of any kind is a self-styled motivating strain. When you are emotional approximately some component you usually tend to get triggered to each enhance it or ruin it simply. Be on top of things of your emotions first. They are the number one gear to gaining inner motivation. Learn the way to use feelings in all the right places. When you're emotional about someone or some component, you may understand that you do now not must placed an excessive amount of strive into making sure that you each acquire them or please them. Keep your emotional health up and taking walks and motivation is certain to return rushing into your vessels.

Right Priority

Control the quantity of relevance you assign to human beings and topics. It is all approximately priorities and the way you pass about setting them all over again. When you have got disordered priorities you simply are going to face disappointments. Disappointments bring about failures, which in turn make you demotivated. Motivating is as social a manner as hundreds as it's miles a personal one. Like we have got visible it stated earlier than, human beings art work in companies. We have usually favored to stay in organizations, be it at the equal time as searching, farming or building. Why ought to motivation be any man or woman of a kind? Become an perception for someone and in flip they will be the equal for a person else. It is a sequence reaction technique. When you skip at the beacon you enlighten and assist a person inside the method putting the way for a hundred others to benefit from the same.

Look on the Bright Side

Learn to see the extreme factor of things. In our madness at things going downhill, we regularly forget about the alternative factor of the meadow. Remember if the bucket is going down a nicely, there may be some other surrender of the rope bobbing up as well. Try seeking out such ropes that get up. Hold directly to them and get out of that properly. Most people are in such wells in our lives. We refuse to take a look at the rope and think of our wells due to the fact the complete global. We accumulate our fates and deny the very lifestyles of some issue referred to as the outer worldwide. Like it's been pressured upon inside the 2d monetary catastrophe itself, see the glass as half of complete and no longer half empty, and in case you are wiser you may drink the damned whiskey and end up a n opportunist however that is beside the issue right here.

Remove Demotivation

There is a distinction amongst lack of motivation and demotivation. When you are demotivated, you're being driven past zero motivation. You are not simply hopeless however moreover pessimistic about your potentialities. However, a lack of motivation is just an absence of motivation that can be crammed on every occasion. Demotivation is worse than loss of motivation for the cause that there can be more room to art work in this situation. Try and paintings on eliminating the demotivating factors for your life. A nagging neighbor, a pessimistic buddy, an over looking beforehand to romantic companion; those are the form of humans that could be tagged as demotivating in nature. Try to every accurate them or stop them.

Declutter Your Life

Decluttering suggests that you are equipped to have your dreams set and clear. You no longer are entwined among cobwebs that surrounded you in clouds of uncertainty. Make topics much less hard and do not complicate topics in which it is not required. Go for shortcut routes in preference to an prolonged reduce which calls for you to spend extra electricity in it.

Have Clear Objectives in Life

First of all, make up a highbrow map of in that you're fame right now and in which you need yourself to be in say 5 years from now. Goal setting, as has been burdened earlier than is an essential issue of person development. When you positioned dreams, you end 1/2 of of your artwork. Setting of dreams allows you smooth the bigger photograph. It does not will can help you live hindered. Obstacles will although be there; best now you could realize which impediment to address and which to stroll by the use of the usage of.

A real warrior is aware about which battles to fight and which to leave. It is not your procedure to fight each battle that comes your manner. Pick your battles; apprehend which reason or what human beings to face for. Motivation is a confined power. You cannot discover the cash for to spend it on matters that don't rely variety as a good buy as others. Remember what Plato as quickly as said. ''I do now not realise the formulae to fulfillment but the formulae to failure is to try to please all and sundry''. Do now not aim to be a people pleaser, specifically at the same time as you're on quick supply of motivation.

www.ingramcontent.com/pod-product-compliance
Lightning Source LLC
Chambersburg PA
CBHW071337120626
46546CB00002B/596